THOUGHT CATALOG BOOKS

The Headache Factory

The Headache Factory

True Tales of Online Obsession and
Madness

JIM GOAD

Thought Catalog Books

Brooklyn, NY

Contents

Introduction

This is, unfortunately, a work of nonfiction. All events described herein are either documented or true to the best of my memory. Except for the Child-Fucking Class Warrior, all stalkers' and harassers' names have been changed because these deliberately intrusive and congenitally worthless walking abortions do not deserve the publicity. The child-fucker deserves the eternal taint. All citations from email and online posts are reprinted with typographical errors intact, because it is not my fault that these schmendricks are illiterate. I've met plenty of nice people online. This book is not about them.

1

The Stalk Market

Oh, what a warm womb the Web provides for the frustrated, the voiceless, the inadequate, the terminally unpleasant, the egregiously untalented, and the grown men taking bong hits in their mothers' basements!

Shrouded by the cyber-cloud and cocooned behind a fake screen name, you can be anyone you want to be on the Internet—especially someone stronger, more attractive, and braver than you are in real life.

The best thing about the Internet is that it allows everyone to express his, her, or its opinion.

That's also the worst thing about it.

It's where everyone can get to know you, no matter whether you want them to or not. It's where everyone is free to harass you from behind a black curtain, regardless of whether you even know them. At least in a comedy club you can see who's heckling you.

When I was but a wee tiny lad, I thought that people were spying on me through the shower nozzle in our bathtub. I used to feel the same way about our TV—I worried whether all the characters onscreen could see me.

Decades later in county jail, I was in an open dormitory of 56 inmates and one guard. There was not one cranny in that entire dorm where everyone couldn't see everyone else at all times. The only spots where there was partial privacy were the two public shower stalls, and even then, everyone could see your head and feet as you soaped yourself. There was no place to hide.

The Internet is like a county-jail dorm for the entire planet. It's where the world spies and snitches on itself. You're all connected through this massive throbbing digital tumor. It has rendered the very notion of privacy a quaint antiquarian relic. It has forever splintered and fractured and broken and shunted the way people deal with one another. With the technology still a mere embryo, no one can fully grasp the social significance of this vast black hole that has taken over our lives and is sucking us into a giant digital vacuum cleaner.

Jean-Paul Sartre said that death is the real hell for existentialists, because that's when others get to define you. The dead no longer have control over their life's meaning, so others feast on their identity like buzzards pecking at a carcass. With the Internet, it's like existential hell, only you haven't died yet. It's *living* hell. The Internet is slowly erasing everyone's internal world. No matter where you are, all the other bees in the hive can see you.

In an atomized society that's crumbling into subatomic particles, the Web serves as a proxy social life for many people, sociopaths among them. The Internet provides everyone, including the lonely and the disturbed, easy and instant access to nearly everyone else on Earth. Technology has encouraged a new bumper crop of obsessive personalities to bloom like so many malignant mushrooms across cyberspace. It allows people to behave like cunts in entirely new ways. It is a grand enabler of assholish behavior, a playground for the malicious.

Human beings always were and always will be idiots. But the Internet allows them to be *instant* idiots.

People, savages that they are, will seek to torture one another with or without technology, but the Web makes it that much easier. Suddenly, the whole world is at the pervert's fingertips. Due to the Web's anonymity, it is fertile ground for stalkers. Most people with any sort of online presence have likely dealt with some degree of creeps and lurkers and faceless harassers.

The Internet is where no one seems real until it's way too late. It is where, sooner or later, everyone will be stalked for at least 15 minutes.

2

Harassholes in Cyberia

"Stalking," like "racism," is a word that is dimly defined and grossly overused.

Some people consider it stalking if you take a peep at a high-school friend's Facebook page. That's a gentle and passive form of *snooping*, but to call it "stalking" is a tad harsh. You aren't invading their personal space because they aren't aware you're doing it.

As I define it, *stalking* involves persistently piercing the personal bubble of someone who has told you to leave them alone. A stalker is someone who feels no shame for invading your personal space like a chest cold inhabits every last bronchiole of your lungs. They are assholes that harass you—*harassholes*. If they are fans that feel snubbed, they are also *fanholes*.

Others define the term more clinically. In 1995, social researchers J. Reid Meloy and Shayna Gothard defined stalking as "an abnormal or long term pattern of threat or harassment directed toward a specific individual."

Wikipedia's page on "cyberstalking" includes a definition by a "technology ethics professor" named Lambèr Royakkers:

> *Stalking is a form of mental assault, in which the perpetrator repeatedly, unwantedly, and disrup-*

tively breaks into the life-world of the victim, with whom he has no relationship (or no longer has), with motives that are directly or indirectly traceable to the affective sphere.

In 1998, researchers Brian Spitzberg and William Cupach defined "obsessive relational intrusion" as:

repeated and unwanted pursuit and invasion of one's sense of physical or symbolic privacy by another person, either stranger [or] acquaintance, who desires and/or presumes an intimate relationship.

Just as I don't understand rape—how can you even get aroused over someone who doesn't want to fuck you?—I can't relate to the idea of bugging and needling and poking at someone who has asked you to leave them alone. I don't go to most of the places where I'm *wanted*, much less anywhere I'm not. On any given day I am typically trying to avoid people rather than befriend them.

I've gained some notoriety as a writer, but only in a microscopic milieu. I am but a lowly neutrino in the vast universe of celebrity. Still, I tend to attract a certain strain of fan that idolizes me to a degree that even I, a brazen megalomaniac who polishes my balls with Turtle Wax, find unrealistic.

If one psychological diagnosis could be applied to nearly everyone who's harassed me over the years, it would be Borderline Personality Disorder. Nearly all of my harassers display a pattern of intense idealization followed by extreme devaluation. One day I'm the Messiah; the next day I'm Satan. This tendency of switching violently from idolatry to demonization is known among headshrinkers as "splitting."

None of my devoted e-harassers is the type who would simply hate me because of my writing or my unsavory public persona. Those people tend to leave me alone.

Nah, these losers fashioned me into a hero and then sought to smash their idol to pieces.

They make direct physical threats, devise elaborate blackmail attempts, and eagerly spread false rumors. Some encourage others to harass me while pestering my friends, employers, and perceived romantic rivals. Others have launched DDoS attacks and engaged in all other manner of electronic tantrum throwing. And in most cases, the most I've done to "provoke" such reactions is gently telling them to go away after they'd started to annoy me.

More than most, I have felt the merciless wrath of the defriended. I have smelled their foul-breathed fury, and yea, it is a stink that passeth all imagination.

Herein I'll detail several cases that would give anyone a headache, but I'd prefer you read this as a sort of grand comedy, an entirely real but seemingly surreal account of how low and petty and cheap and cowardly people can act when they hold the joystick and you are an easy target.

3

High-Profile Stalkers of Yore

In 1972 a paranoid bespectacled loner named Arthur Bremer shot Alabama governor and presidential candidate George Wallace, crippling both Wallace and his presidential aspirations. Bremer's mind had slowly unspooled following a romantic rejection, so he began keeping a diary and plotting his attack. He was allegedly the inspiration for the 1976 film *Taxi Driver*, in which Robert De Niro portrays Travis Bickle, a Vietnam vet who stalks a presidential candidate, then goes on a shooting spree to salvage the honor of a 12-year-old street tart played by Jodie Foster.

Foster unwittingly played a role in the 1981 assassination attempt on President Ronald Reagan by the chubby narcissistic schizoid loner and failed songwriter John Hinckley. After becoming fixated on *Taxi Driver,* Hinckley formed a delusional romantic attachment to Jodie Foster. Failing in several attempts to capture her attention and win her affection, Hinckley decided he could only become her "equal" by achieving Foster's level of fame—albeit via a televised presidential shooting instead of reciting lines on the silver screen. After wounding Reagan and others, Hinckley wrote that he had given Foster "the greatest love offering in the history of the world." He successfully copped an insanity plea and was wheeled away to a mental hospital rather than prison.

The most famous case of a fatal celebrity obsession was 1980's murder of John Lennon by Mark David Chapman, a former Beatles fan who made it his mission to punish Lennon for perceived moral transgressions. Chapman, a born-again Christian, was allegedly incensed that Lennon once claimed The Beatles were "more popular than Jesus." He also said that Lennon was a hypocrite for singing "imagine no possessions" while flitting about the world like an aristocratic fop. Inspired by the novel *The Catcher in the Rye*, Chapman made it his mission to exterminate Lennon's "phoniness."

One of the most persistent celebrity stalkers was Margaret Mary Ray, arrested eight times for trespassing on TV talk-show host David Letterman's property, including an incident where she stole his Porsche. Ms. Ray would serve nearly three years in jail and mental hospitals as a result of stalking Letterman. In 1998, she killed herself by kneeling in front of an oncoming train.

In 1990, TV actress Rebecca Schaeffer was murdered by a brooding, apelike male fan who'd been stalking her for three years. He was apparently enraged that she'd become "another Hollywood whore" after she appeared in a bed scene with a man.

Around the same time, actress Sharon Gless was nearly killed by a lesbian stalker who'd barricaded herself in Gless's Hollywood mansion with a rifle and 500 rounds of ammo.

In 1994, singer Sarah McLachlan took passages from letters a Canadian male stalker had sent her and turned them into lyrics for her song "Possession." The stalker, Uwe Vandrei, sued McLachlan for using his words as lyrics. He admitted that the only reason he filed the lawsuit was because it would enable him to be near her physically, even if in a courtroom. Before the trial started, Vandrei was dead from an apparent suicide.

In 1996, Florida pest-control officer Ricardo López mailed a sulfuric-acid-rigged letter bomb to Icelandic female singer Björk, with whom he'd been obsessed for years. He then videotaped himself sticking a gun in his mouth and pulling the trigger.

Actress Ashley Tisdale was recently stalked by a man who made repeated attempts at contact that included Tweeting violent song lyrics at her and showing up at her house pretending to be a pizza deliveryman.

Actor Hugh Jackman claims to have been stalked by an obsessed female fan who in April 2013 allegedly threw an electric razor filled with her own pubic hair at him.

People have been raped and killed by those who first tried to reach out and touch them online. The king of social media, Facebook's Mark Zuckerberg, was forced to take legal action against a delusional stalker.

An obsessed fan recently scared actress Patricia Arquette off Facebook. Arquette says she made herself accessible on Facebook to see if celebrities and fans were able to become friends:

> *The experiment was, Could a celebrity actually friend strangers and get to know them as a person? Just a regular person? Could you really become friends? Could you move past all that they*

had in their mind about you and actually show them the real you? Could you get to know the real them a little? I would say on a large part yes. A beautiful and sweet yes....However, apparently 10 days or so that all changed.

4

Ladies & Gentlemen, Rupert Pupkin!

The word "fanatic" starts with the word "fan." A certain malignant breed of fan seems to presume that since they "know" you through your work, they're entitled to a personal relationship with you for life—and if you refuse, you must be destroyed.

In addition to *Taxi Driver*, Hollywood portrayed stalkers in films such as *Play Misty for Me* and *Fatal Attraction*. Both flicks involved romantically obsessed females, with *Misty* adding the star-struck angle of a woman who stalks a radio DJ played by Clint Eastwood.

But the *ne plus ultra*, the *crème de la crème*, the absolute pinnacle and apogee and apex and mountaintop of cinematic stalking movies is 1983's *The King of Comedy*, which like *Taxi Driver* stars Robert De Niro and was directed by Martin Scorsese.

De Niro portrays Rupert Pupkin, a socially hobbled autograph hound and wannabe standup comic who forms an unhealthy obsession over late-night talk-show host Jerry Langford, played by comedian Jerry Lewis. (At the time of the filming, Lewis had been dealing with a real-life stalker who'd been terrorizing him and his family for years.)

Rupert's repeated failed attempts to break into show business by making Jerry listen to his comedy routine escalate in desperation. When Rupert shows up unannounced at Jerry's weekend house, Jerry finally threatens to call the police unless Rupert leaves. Rupert vows revenge:

> **Rupert:** *I'm gonna work 50 times harder, and I'm gonna be 50 times more famous than you.*
>
> **Jerry:** *Then you're gonna have idiots like you plaguing your life!*

After this humiliating face-to-face rejection, Rupert kidnaps Jerry and holds him hostage until network executives allow Rupert to perform his stand-up routine on Jerry's show. While a gun is held to Jerry's head, Rupert admonishes him that "friendship is a two-way street" and "I'd hate to have to do anything drastic."

Throughout *The King of Comedy*, Rupert's real-life losses and loneliness are punctuated by fantasy sequences where he and Jerry are showbiz equals.

Back in the real world, Rupert is sent to prison for kidnapping Jerry. In the film's final scene he is released from prison to become a best-selling author and highly successful standup comic. What's unclear is whether or not this happy ending is only occurring in Rupert's head.

5

Sweet Gene's Suicide Attempt

My first brush with a deranged fan was by proxy. It involved a female-to-male transsexual who made it his life's mission to form a close personal relationship with Rolling Stones singer Mick Jagger.

I lived in Hollywood from 1987-1994, and my home phone number was only one digit different from that of Capitol Records. People trying to reach Capitol would wrongly dial me all the time. When I moved to Oregon late in 1994, I had the LA number forwarded to my new one in Oregon.

As a self-proclaimed Stones fanatic since the mid-60s, the weak-voiced little bipolar female-to-male tranny that called himself "Sweet Gene" should have known that the band never recorded for Capitol Records. But he mistakenly dialed my old Hollywood number and then was forwarded to my new one in Oregon.

Gene was far from stable—he was sometimes euphoric and sometimes suicidal, sometimes a man and sometimes a woman. Only one constant emerged through it all—he fucking LOVED Mick Jagger. He had loved the puffy-lipped rock god since reaching some unarticulated epiphany in 1966, which at the time he began calling my Oregon number translated into roughly THIRTY YEARS of unrequited love.

I picture Gene at a Stones concert, one fiber in a carpet of other nobodies, a tiny delusional flea watching the big dogs onstage, knowing that one day he and Mick will meet, fall in love, and tra-la-la their way into a sexually freaky dotage.

At first, I tried explaining to Gene that it was a wrong number and that I was neither a friend nor a representative of Mick Jagger's.

But Gene kept calling.

So I grabbed a tape recorder and decided to have some fun with him. At first I called as "Mr. Fischmann," a self-described "press liaison for the Rolling Stones," asking Gene whether he'd be willing to wait by the phone a few minutes for Mick's call.

That would be no problem. Gene had been waiting his whole life.

Then I called as "Mick," doing a Jagger impression so awful that you can hear me laughing at my own impersonation. After agreeing to meet Gene the next time a tour brought the Stones through town, Mick tells Gene to "call anytime."

The calls started coming with metronomic regularity, sometimes a dozen a day, the pitch of Gene's voice varying wildly depending on where he was on the manic-depressive roller coaster.

After a week of such sonic assaults, I popped a cassette of "Tumbling Dice" into my boom box and called as "Keith Richards," shouting over the music that the band was in Japan getting ready to go onstage but that Gene shouldn't worry and Mick would call as soon as he got back in the States.

Gene made more calls and more calls and more calls after that. And after he was done with those, he called some more.

The next prank call came from "Red Sovine," a beefy-sounding "security guard for the Rolling Stones Corporation," browbeating Gene about the alleged death threats he'd been making to Mick.

A few days later, Gene got a call from "Morty Feinberg," an "entertainment lawyer for the Rolling Stones Corporation," apologizing for the "*meshuga goy* bodyguard" who'd been so rude to Gene over the phone. After some rudimentary probing into Gene's sexuality (when asked about his sex change, Gene explains, "I didn't like being penetrated—I wanted to do the penetrating"), Morty promises that Mick will call in a few days.

He never did. A planned phone-sex call from "Mick" was aborted after Gene attempted suicide.

The messages leading up to Gene's decision to swallow a bottle of Klonopin in despair that Mick hadn't called are among the grimmest audio tracks you'll ever hear. And the ones he leaves after eating the pills, with his voice fading into near incomprehensibility, are positively soul-flattening.

A social worker left a message the next morning, explaining that after Gene was rushed to the hospital and rescued from death, he asked her to call Mick and tell him not to feel guilty about it.

Back from the hospital, Gene said that while on the operating table, he heard a voice ("I think it was God speaking to me...there was no one in the room") saying that "there's always a tomorrow," and he wanted to know whether there would be a tomorrow for him and Mick.

To Gene, his near-death experience transformed "the beautiful Mick Jagger" from a mere celebrity god to a god of a higher level, a sanctified being who is "not the Devil" even though he might have been possessed of the Devil years ago when he recorded that Devil song.

The remaining messages, a bleak Klieg light cast on the crushing loneliness of a scared little she-man, are nearly unbearable to hear. Gene still believes Mick is trying to call him, but because of physical pain, he's unable to get out of bed and answer quickly enough. He sends Mick a crystal ball, a portrait he drew of Jagger, and even a picture of himself. He says all his gifts were sent back, presumably by the record company.

Gene continued calling for years, losing touch only after I moved again and neglected to forward my number.

It was a tragicomic odyssey of a stalker-fan even creepier than Rupert Pupkin in *The King of Comedy*, because Gene was real, however divorced from reality he was.

6

My Salad Days as a Psycho

If you search my name online, you may quickly form the impression that I am not a nice person. That's not entirely true. If I like you, I can be as sweet as sugar cream pie. But you need to understand two things:

- I am not like most people.

- I don't like most people.

Nice or not, I would never claim to be a *normal* person. Many people pride themselves for being "different" in superficial ways such as musical tastes, political views, and what they choose to do with their procreative organs. I'm different in the most meaningful sense—inside the head. I'm an epileptic and a survivor of a huge brain tumor, so I'd wager there's something a bit "off-brand" about my wiring. I'm working from a different kind of motherboard than most people are. I'm not *trying* to be weird; it's that I couldn't be normal if I tried.

While most people are guided by what's popular and unpopular, I'm fixated on what's true and false. I couldn't care less whether you like me, but it's extremely important that you *understand* me. You could insult me to my face for a solid half-hour, and the only thing—beyond your halitosis—that would bother me is if you got any of your facts wrong. Social approval means nothing to me, while honesty means everything. And you don't get popular by being honest.

The neurological *hoi polloi* would say that makes me a cold-hearted robotic narcissistic sociopath with a lemon twist of Asperger's, but what do they know?

As a highly abnormal person, I have not led a normal life. I was recently sharing some real-life stories with my friend Nick, who's a walking encyclopedia of strange arcana. He said, "Jimbo, I believe everything you're telling me here. It's just that *I've never heard stories like this before.*"

But as weird as my life as been, it never seems to get *less* weird.

Nearly twenty years ago an English professor at Berkeley cited an issue of my self-published magazine *ANSWER Me!*—the fourth and final installment, the notorious "Rape Issue"—as evidence of an author who showed signs of Post-traumatic Stress Disorder. I think she was right. She saw a raw agony that others had misinterpreted as a clumsy attempt to shock. For better or worse, she saw that the pain and anger were real rather than a pose.

I never stalked her.

The ones I went after—and I *really* went after them—were other zine publishers who mocked the idea that I was truly as violent and angry as I portrayed myself. If they expressed a wisp of doubt, I made sure they'd get a taste of my rage that was hot enough to scar their tongues.

Psychotic? Yes. Sincere? Absolutely.

As I see it, I was the *opposite* of a troll. I was so angered by the idea that I was only trolling, I'd threaten to kill people who suggested as much.

There was a punk-rock zine in LA written by rich-kid poseurs who in a review accused me of being a rich-kid poseur. I harassed them by phone until they shit their last pair of silk diapers.

There was a trash-culture zine by a blubbery New York porn addict who also insinuated I may have been faking the anger. I sent him a letter via Certified Mail written in my own blood.

I continued with these antics for about three years, almost all while I was publishing *ANSWER Me!* As I saw it, I was defending myself, and it didn't matter who got hurt in the process...even myself. At the time it all seemed noble and righteous to me.

At the height of my popularity as a writer, I was a truly dangerous individual who wouldn't blink at the thought of killing anyone who mocked me. I quickly garnered a reputation as someone not to be fucked with unless you wished to be fucked back a thousand times harder. When it became common knowledge that I was every bit as unhinged as I'd claimed, there was nothing left for me to prove.

In my salad days as a psycho, the stunts I pulled were often more extreme than any of the stories I'm about to share. But my blasts of vengeance were far briefer than those of the intruders, harassers, party crashers, and discarded anal prolapses you're about to meet. The dynamic was also different in that I had never been fans of my targets and never sought their friendship. I was merely on a psychotic quest to convince unbelievers that I was psychotic.

But I also received enough attention that I started attracting stalkers of my own. I had screamed at the world, and the world belched psychosis back in my face.

Sometimes I think Hitler would have been better served if he claimed he'd just been trolling.

7

All My Little Rupert Pupkins

In over 20 years of publishing, I've been stalked and harassed by multiple damaged and pathetic personages.

All of them were fans of mine. Or at least they were until I ignored or blocked them. Just as when you dump a girl, her estimation of your dick size shrinks by four inches, apparently you immediately lose all your talent once you tell someone to go away.

My mangy menagerie of readers-turned-stalkers is vast and dedicated. Sometimes sitting at a computer feels like punching the time clock at a headache factory. It's like an endless loop of really bad breakups with people whom I never dated.

After a while, the only part that's not tedious is whether an individual antagonist brings any new moves to the demented martial art that is electronic stalking.

But mostly they practice the same old predictable *katas* in rigid lockstep.

On the front end, before they get intrusive or annoying enough that I ask them to leave me alone, all of them claim to know what's best for me far better than even I do. They're only trying to help. They pride themselves for belonging to an elite few who "understand" and "get" me.

But their behavior after I snub them proves they never understood a word I wrote.

Because their lives are typically an uninterrupted streak of losses, "winning" becomes paramount to them. They will not rest until they feel they've defeated me.

They want to make clear that if I'm going to reject them, well, sir, they're going to reject me back HARDER.

Nearly all of them engage in psychological projection to varying degrees, most often accusing anyone but themselves of being "fanboys" and "stalkers."

Many will harass me for years with absolutely no response on my part, yet they'll claim that *I'm* the obsessed one who can't leave them alone.

Several of them will immediately try and ingratiate themselves with anyone else they perceive as my enemy, urging others to share sob stories and plot revenge as part of Jim Goad's Broken Hearts Club Band.

They will also poke their beaks into the business of everyone with whom I am on good terms—friends, family members, employers—seeking to either defame me or air their side of the "story."

They exaggerate their involvement in my life, taking credit for introducing me to others I'd known for years and for stealing ideas they never had in the first place.

They believe everything I write is aimed at them. They think we are locked in some life-or-death battle, when usually the only thing I do beyond documenting their stalking is to ignore them.

They'll do the most unforgivable things, but if they apologize and I don't forgive them, suddenly *I'm* the asshole.

Even though they are the only ones creating drama and making things ugly, they will insist they're tired of all the drama and don't want things to get ugly.

If I show any reaction to their needling, no matter how tame, they've "touched a nerve." If I don't react, they call me a coward.

And when I invariably cut the cord, all of them see fit to loudly proclaim how "over" it they are. They will repeatedly claim it in case you didn't hear them the first hundred thousand times.

It is coldly fascinating to watch them struggling to mend and patch and sculpt and glue and tape and reconstruct and primer and repaint their shattered egos.

I never knew that physical frailty or "mental illness" gives one *carte blanche* to engage in all sorts of premeditated malicious behavior. Many of these freaks will have flashes of insight and send apologetic emails blaming their behavior on a medical condition. One of them said he'd neglected to take his experimental psychiatric pills. Another blamed it on abnormally high ammonia levels due to Hepatitis C. Yet another claimed his vengeful cyber-antics were due to being recently diagnosed with bowel cancer.

Many of them appear to feel invincible in the sense that my criminal record makes me legally vulnerable, so they feel as if they can take shot after shot without repercussions. It's like they're poking a caged animal with sticks yet somehow manage to feel brave about it.

They are all fixated far more on what they perceive as my persona or public image than they are on my writing. They seem blind to the fact that only thing that would actually shame me is to point out factual errors or logical flaws in what I write. Instead, they go on campaigns to "expose" something real, imagined, or highly exaggerated about my personal life that is intended to publicly humiliate or silence me. Yet it never hurts.

I gradually realized that whatever they fling at me is almost always the sort of thing that would hurt *them* rather than me. The moment I do nothing more than dispassionately document their behavior, they cry foul, scream that I'm libeling or defaming them, and demand that my every mention of them be instantly scrubbed from the Web forever. They feel entirely entitled to dish out a seven-course meal of abuse but scream to high heaven if I answer back with so much as a dinner mint.

They talk mountains of shit but can't STAND the idea of having people "talk shit" about them. That's a constant among them—the very phrase "talking shit." They *all* use it. They cannot BEAR to have anyone "talk shit" about them. They vow eternal vengeance if the shit-talking doesn't immediately cease so they can get back to their full-time job, which is to talk shit about me.

In contrast, if someone talks shit about me, I cut them out of my life and don't send them a Christmas card. Seems easier.

Breaking up is hard to do—for them at least. For me, it's easy. That is, until they make it hard.

8

The Stalker Who Put Me in Prison

Though I have written four books and roughly one million published words at this point, some people would prefer that I be known only for hitting my girlfriend and going to prison because of it.

If I stopped shooting heroin 15 years ago, most people would not still consider me a junkie.

But if I hit a woman 15 years ago—and mind you, I hit her *back*—well, I will remain subhuman forever. And although my crime had nothing to do with deception and I've always been completely honest about it, for some people this eternally demolishes my credibility. You can't believe a word I say. There's no possible way I'm correct if write that it's 72 degrees outside today...even (or especially) if it's actually 72 degrees outside today. If Charles Manson told you the sky was blue, then obviously it's red.

In an increasingly dumb and hyperemotional world, people seem incapable of comprehending that *argumentum ad hominem* does not substitute for a logical refutation. And if you don't understand what I just wrote there, you're part of the problem, you STUPID motherfucker.

The entire tragic, psychotic, and mutually bloody romantic

situation that landed me in the pokey eats up about half of my book *Shit Magnet*. During the year I was with the girl who became known as "the 21-year-old stripper," I kept all of my lunatic paramour's voicemail messages. Here are some of her more "energetic" ones:

> *I want to fucking castrate you, I want to stab you a million times all over your fucking body....So, I hate your guts, and I'm going to kill you, and I don't care what happens to you or your fucking wife, and I hope you die.*
> —1:02 PM, Wednesday, September 3, 1997

> *I hate your FUCKING guts and I want to RIP YOU APART and DESTROY every fucking living cell in your body. I want to CRUSH YOU and take tweezers and pull out your FUCKING NIPPLES, and cut you up into a million pieces and scratch out your eyes and I want to chop off your FUCK-ING HEAD.*
> —8:13 PM, Wednesday, September 24, 1997

> *Hi, it's me, and I was just saying it might be necessary, ASAP, for you to take out some restraining order against me. Seriously, Jim, I'm infected with you....I don't know any other way to describe it. I can't get over this, I can't wash it off me, I'm insane, that's all I can think about, I am so obsessed and possessive of you....I'll go to extreme lengths to capture you, you better restrain me, and we both know what I'm capable of. I mean, you've*

threatened to call the police many times, so let's get this filthy rotten piece of garbage out of your life once and for all.
—10:13 AM, February 6, 1998

[Tight, sneering voice] *Hi, lovey-dovey who always wants to be near me and would never cheat on me, you fucking asshole. You better be there in 20 minutes, or a fucking rock is going through your landlord's fucking window. And if you ain't there, I don't care. If your landlord lets me in, I'm throwing away, every hour that you're gone, I'm throwing away all your ANSWER Me! magazines, all your letters, destroying your house, and this ain't gonna be a fun night for you, boy, 'cause I'm not in a good mood. And I'm destroying everything you fuckin' own. So you can even have the cops there, because I'm not gonna play quiet when you're not there in 20 minutes. You're having a rock through your fucking window. And if your fucking landlord doesn't answer the phone, or lets me in, then I'm destroying every single possession you own. So be there in 20 minutes or get FUCKED!*
—7:39 PM, March 22, 1998

Did she come by and pick you up? How sweet! Listen, Goad, I know for a fact that you're not home. I've just been all around your fucking house, the whole perimeter, I've surveyed it, the inside, and

out, and I couldn't get on your roof but I rang the chimes, I know for a fucking fact that you're not there, buddy, the game is up, so get your stuff, have her drop you off, 'cause I ain't leaving the premises.
—8:44 PM, April 11, 1998

Darling, where are we at, the Farmhouse? Ah, darling, you know what? I ain't gonna wait for that olive branch, 'cause I don't want it. You know what I was hoping for? That it would be you. But it's not, and you have destroyed my dreams....You are going to dispose of me...and you're not going to be able to get rid of me so easy. There's going to be...somebody's going to wind up dead, whether it's me or you. And don't think [laughs] that I won't find a way. Don't think, for even a second, that you can get away. And I wouldn't be very sloppy about it, believe me. If you hurt me bad enough, you will be fuckin' blown to fuckin' pieces. You will be assassinated. And there is no way, unless you never want to make a public appearance again, that that's going to...ah...uh, I'm going to follow you, I'm going to find out where—you are a fuckin' famous personality. I'm going to find out where you are, and I'm going to blow your brains to fuckin' smither-fuckin'-reens!...Your head—it's going to be out of this fucking universe. Your head's going to be blown to fucking shreds. You better pick up the fucking

phone.
—8:29 PM, April 13, 1998

I am such a masochist—I really want to go to jail, so please hand this tape over to the police and tell them I'm calling you, I'm violating the restraining order, it's 10:15 PM and I really really really need to go to jail. So have them over here as soon as possible, 'cause I'm ready to go back, 'cause I have nothing to do on the outside. So, if you could do that for me, love of my FUCKING life, I would really appreciate it. I really want to go back there. And that way you could just fuck your brains out and have no problem, you know, with what's going on, even though I'm working on your goddamned BIRTHDAY present right now. I can't stay away from you, I'm gonna have to be behind bars, so go ahead and do what you will, Jim Goad.
—10:18 PM, May 6, 1998

All the way through our irredeemably sick year, she taunted and stalked and threatened and scratched and punched me into finally hitting her back. During a videoconference with my lawyer while I was in jail, I described her as a fan who became a lover who became a stalker.

Over the course of our massively dysfunctional yearlong relationship, I had many chances to get Miss Lyin' locked up for physically attacking me and threatening my life. Evil monster that I am, I couldn't manage to be that coldhearted. I can lose my temper and punch someone, but I can't consign them to a cage. But the first chance she had to get me locked up, I was shipped Special Delivery to the human warehouse. She even gloated that with me in jail, at least no other girls could fuck me.

I will go to my grave believing in my bone marrow she was the predator in that saga. Still, my lack of remorse tends to make people think I'm despicable rather than honest. If I were a social animal, I'd apologize even if I didn't mean it. But I'd rather be honest than popular. It's that faulty Aspergery wiring of mine again.

I've never apologized for what I did because I don't feel sorry about it. Unlike most people, who've likely never experienced physical beatings or incarceration in their antiseptically trauma-free lives, I can see the situation from both sides. I've had my face bashed in far worse than she got it that morning at 5AM, when most members of the "society" to whom I supposedly owe a perpetual "debt" were likely asleep. And I also wound up spending nearly 29 months in various state-run dog kennels because of it, which is far worse than taking a few shots to the head.

I have a lawyer friend who was a federal public defender in death-penalty cases. He typically defended multi-murdering gangbangers and serial-killing rapists who'd cram their victims' cunts full of Fisher-Price toys. He says that Anne Lyin' was one of the most dangerous individuals he'd ever seen and that she shouldn't even be walking the streets.

For all I know, she may not be anymore.

About two years into my prison bid, she wound up purposely running over a bicyclist with her car. She fled the scene and failed to appear in court for a hearing. She eventually pled guilty to a felony but only did two months in county jail.

But since she has a slit between her legs, she will never have to deal with the stigma that I do. People were outraged that I had used my superior size and strength against her, despite the fact that the blood evidence and my mug shot verify that she'd hit me first that morning. I'm 5'11" and at the time weighed 155 pounds. She was 5'9" and weighed 135. Still, they were outraged—*far* more than they were to hear that she'd used a 4,000-pound car to run over a presumably medium-sized human bicyclist.

But you should never hit a woman, went the blind mantra.

Right. Because your pseudo-religious indignation really has nothing to do with the idea that one shouldn't strike back against physically smaller and weaker opponents. It's because women's bodies are deemed more sacred in this society. So for the love of the resurrected Jesus Christ flying around on butterfly wings sprinkling pixie dust and blowing rainbow bubbles with a magic wand, at least knock off the horseshit about some imaginary "war against women" and females being "second-class citizens." They have the law's full iron weight—and the culture's automatic sympathy—on their side, which are much more brutal weapons than any fist.

Fearing that she'd try to contact me or frame me for a crime upon my release, I applied to serve my three years of parole in Illinois but was refused. Shortly before I got out of prison I had a dream that I was standing in a bathroom peeing. Looking out through a small, eye-level window, I saw Anne grinning in maniacally at me from outside. I knew she'd try to contact me again.

Upon my release, a friend had set me up with a Yahoo! discussion group where I'd field questions from readers. Less than a month after I got out, I spent a weekend camping with a woman in the Columbia River Gorge. When I returned to Portland on Sunday night, I found that Anne Lyin' had crashed my Yahoo! group and was gleefully smearing her verbal menses everywhere. Since I was under legal restrictions to have no contact with her, I had to shut the group down.

She started her own Yahoo! group and sent out a mass email to members of my group. Its subject line was:

Join my club or I'll NEVER stop stalking you!

Despite having played the role of passive victim to the press, she continued boasting of her violent streak:

I love that I've actually shouted at two different chicks two days in a row, "YA WANNA GET HIT, BITCH??!"...oh yeah, and smashed some convenient store owner's display case down, too...Having a tough time keeping my cool, but the courts didn't recommend angry management, that's cuz the experts all know I'm sane.

Mere months after doing jail time for running over someone with her car, she was bragging to the world about trying to run over a group of girls in a parking lot:

She and her sixteen-year-old accomplices found it quite amusing when she looked at me and said,

"Woof!" as they waltzed past my parked vehicle...I was laughing too, a few seconds later, upon seeing the horrified expressions across their baby-fat faces after I started the ignition and floored the gas, aiming right for the chick who made the remark...They were smart puppies, though, and dodged outta the way.

She openly admitted to stalking and attacking me—even to falsely accusing me of rape:

What the fuck else do you want from me???? I've owned up to EVERYTHING!!!!Sure, I attacked him numerous times before that fateful morning, threatened him with death, stalked him, fantasized about killing him on a daily basis..Even was fucking glad when he went top jail at first not only cuz I felt safe, but yeah, also so he couldnt fuck anyone else (THATS sick and WRONG)...And yeah, ithink i even told the cops on 5-3 that he raped me...technically, he didn't....

She also claimed that no one, not even family members, believed her story that she didn't hit me first that fateful morning.

Though she had diligently tried to "expose" me for every possible embarrassing detail—real and fabricated—of my life by blasting it online and to whatever media outlet would listen to her, she acted as if she'd been ass-raped when a national magazine revealed that she'd eaten my dog's shit and spit it in my face:

> *Ok, now let's talk about shit eating and piss drinking since it seems it will be FOREVER rubbed in my face …. in HUGE letters in a national magazine "[Anne Lyin'] SHOVED DROPPINGS OF GOAD'S CHIHUAHUA … " How the FUCK do you think that made me feel??? You can't even fathom…Praying when-you meet someone, a boss, coworker, friend's mother, that they won't recognize you as "The shit-eating girl" … The intent of that article was obviously to destroy me…*

She even admitted that she still harbored fantasies of killing me:

> **1/8/01 10:30 pm**
> *Insane Anne Posse (Me and the Voices)*
>
> *Kill Jim.*

A woman of many moods, she also confessed to being remorse-stricken for having me locked away:

> *… Jim, I cried rivers for you last Christmas, not for selfish, stalkerish reasons, but b/c sitting on the couch over at debbies* [my ex-wife] *i looked over at tyco* [my Chihuahua] *and it tore me up that you couldnt be near him and you were locked in*

that horrible place...despite everything, i do regret sending you to prison. If i had it to do again, I wouldn't.

Jim... i'd like to wish you and yours a merry motherfucking Christmas

from me and mine.....

Peace.

These were the words of someone who had seven-and a half months to drop charges while I waited in jail before taking a plea bargain. It was a little too late for apologies and *way* too late to make peace.

I had figured the lurid details of my incarceration would sorely impede my post-prison dating prospects. I couldn't have been more wrong. In a society awash with slack-shouldered, self-castrating, armpit-shaving, testicle-exfoliating, beta-male feminists, I found it amusing if slightly depressing that being a well-known impenitent woman-beater was like catnip to the ladies.

About three months after my release, I shacked up with a heavily tattooed rockabilly girl named **Methrissa**. She was in her early 20s; I was 39. She had a short spiky peroxided hairdo and a malevolent *Clockwork Orange* gleam in her eye. She also had a habit of going into epileptic seizures at the most inconvenient times, such as during sex. I would be told later that she might have been shooting meth the whole time I was with her.

Two weeks after we started seeing one another, she had my name tattooed on her wrist. Four months later, I stupidly had her name tattooed on my bicep. I would eventually try to get her name covered up with a tattoo of thorns and roses, but the cover-up got infected, so my left arm now features a flaming heart with what looks like a dog turd over it.

One Friday night in the spring of 2001 Methrissa and I had a disagreement, so we split off and she went out on the town with her friends while I cruised a couple local bars with my friend Josh from prison.

When I got home around 2 AM, I walked up on the front porch to see that Methrissa had taken all her pictures of me, torn them to pieces, and taped them outside the door.

Not a good sign. *Definitely* not a good sign.

Even though I'd never so much as raised my voice to her, she began making threatening comments about how she "didn't want to have to" send me back to prison. Suddenly I found myself trapped and unsure how to escape this latest catastrophic afterbirth of a romance.

One morning that summer I awoke to tell her I was leaving for good. Rather than letting me go gently, she called the police. My biggest post-prison nightmare—a false accusation—was coming true. While the cops were on their way, she also called up some ex-Nazi skinheads who'd become greasers and asked them to stomp the shit out of me.

When police arrived, they heard both our stories. A cop pulled me aside and said he could tell which one of us was acting hysterically, but since I was on parole, it was probably best that I pack a bag and quietly get out of there. I did, leaving my little pug puppy behind with Methrissa.

It took a half-hour to get to downtown Portland, where for a month I would sleep on the floor in the office of the porno magazine where I worked. When I got into the office, I called my boss, who'd given me the puppy for my 40th birthday. Before I could explain anything, he told me Methrissa had already called him. She'd insinuated that I'd been beating the dog as well as her. He told me not to worry, that he realized how much I loved that puppy and that she was obviously lying.

I desperately tried getting in contact with my parole officer to no avail. Knowing that Methrissa, if she was anything like Anne, would call back soon sobbing her eyes out and apologizing, I went to Radio Shack and purchased equipment to tape her phone calls.

Within 12 hours, she started calling. Fearing a revocation of my parole, I very calmly guided the conversation to ensure that she elucidated quite clearly from every possible angle that I hadn't hit her. She admitted she lied to the cops and was only angry that I was dumping her.

But I still couldn't get ahold of my parole officer and was starting to panic. And Methrissa kept begging for me to come back home. I told her that after what she'd done, it wasn't my home anymore.

After three days of her begging, I agreed that Methrissa could come downtown to talk with me as long as she brought the puppy with her.

The porno-mag office was a floor above a club called Dante's, where a foulmouthed hideous lesbian rapper who calls herself Peaches was scheduled to perform that evening to a standing-room-only crowd. As I stood outside waiting for

Methrissa to arrive, who should walk out of the club chatting with Peaches but Anne Lyin', the stalker who put me in prison?

It had been three years since I saw her, and she walked up to cheerfully ask me how I was doing. Her mien was as casual as if we were coworkers and she hadn't expected to see me at the show.

I looked away and told the bouncer that I was legally bound to have no contact with this woman and that he would be my witness.

Anne went back into the club. When Methrissa got there, I told her the deal. She'd known Anne, who'd fucked Methrissa's brother Saul. She winced at Anne's very name. She said she once saw Anne sitting on the ground as a circle of gutterpunks jerked off onto her face. She also said she once saw Anne fellating a dog.

I wound up having to break up a catfight between a girl who'd *sent* me to prison and one who'd just tried sending me *back* to prison. Methrissa and I took the puppy and walked down to the Portland waterfront, where we sat on a bench in front of the Willamette River.

"I just wanted to kill her for what she'd done to you," Methrissa said.

I didn't say it out loud, but I was thinking that at least I'd committed a crime against Anne. Methrissa had tried to get me jailed merely for breaking up with her.

After five days, I finally was able to get in touch with my parole officer. She said Methrissa had called her claiming I'd been beating her for months. I then played her the tapes where Methrissa admits repeatedly that I'd never laid a finger on her. My PO apologized profusely. The rest of my parole was a breeze.

About a week after talking to my PO, I ran into one of the greaser assassins at a local club. A 6'4" ex-Army Ranger, he was known around town as Salty Dave.

Dave said we needed to go outside. When we got out to the sidewalk, he asked what had happened between me and Methrissa. I told him the story and said, "Dave, you could try to kick my ass and would probably succeed, but I'm *not* going to apologize because I didn't do anything wrong."

Dave eyed me up and down, then asked if he could buy me a drink. He later told a friend that our face-off outside the club was like talking to Clint Eastwood. He said of all the guys in town who pretend they're badasses, he'd finally found a real one.

I saw Anne one more time, again in downtown Portland. I was walking up Burnside Street hand-in-hand with a girl named **Screamy** when I noticed that someone in a pickup truck at a stop sign was smiling at me. After focusing my eyes, I muttered, "Oh, shit—*that's Anne Lyin'.*" Anne stopped smiling, gave me the finger, and then screeched into traffic so loudly I jumped a half-foot off the ground.

Screamy and I lasted about a year and lived together for the final few months. Having grown sick of her kicking me in my shins and spitting in my face and screaming at me on public sidewalks, I sent her packing back to mommy's house. She wasn't worth the legal risk. What I neglected to do was get her apartment key back from her, or at least change the locks.

About two weeks later, she busted in on me and a girl named Jaime a mere 15 seconds or so after we'd finished having sex. Screamy chased Jaime down the apartment-building hallway, then came back at me in full-blown rip-snorting jealous-woman mode. She found Jaime's backpack and began throwing her belongings out the window. She hurled my glass coffee pot at the floor. My pug sat shivering in the corner, terrified.

"You know, I could have you arrested just for being here," I told her. "This is trespassing."

"Go ahead and call the cops," she taunted. "We'll see which one they believe."

Ahh, beautiful. Yet another girl committing crimes—Methrissa had lied to the cops and now Screamy was trespassing in my apartment—and using my "felon" card against me without blinking. It seemed to be their first instinct.

Screamy then took the mattress that I'd tainted by having sex with Jaime, dragged it out of my apartment, down a flight of stairs, and into the apartment-building parking lot.

During the year Screamy and I had been together, I had three violent encounters with a local anti-racist skinhead gang who had convinced themselves that I was a Nazi who once wrote about "beating the Jew" out of my wife. Although untrue, it didn't impede them from their holy mission. The truth never impedes brainwashed morons on holy missions. I wrote about the situation for *VICE* magazine in an article called "Skinheads Against White People." Rumor went out that after the article was published, they put out a contract on my life.

Screamy is mentioned as my "Jewish girlfriend" in that article, but at the time I wrote it, I had a *new* Jewish girlfriend named **Bedwetta**. As the story was told to me, Bedwetta's deceased dad had been one of the wealthiest pimps on the West Coast and her mom was one of his hookers that she'd impregnated.

We lasted nearly a year. When I told her I intended to start seeing Jaime again, Bedwetta threatened to call the cops and lie to them that I'd raped her. When I finally broke up with her, she sent me a barrage of harassing text messages:

> *Poor excvse for a human.* [oct 18,
> 2004...3:04AM]

> *Liar...Loser... Wake up and go to the shrink, you*
> *fucking little freak* [oct 18, 2004...10:59AM]

I only responded once, to text her this:

> *You'll never know how truly sorry I am that things*
> *didn't work out between us.* [oct 18,
> 2004...11:26AM]

She continued:

> *Ill NEVER believe you...BTW—you're SO fucking*
> *depressing. I'm shocked i haven't ended my life*
> *after eleven horrid, wasted months with a piece of*
> *crap, like you.* [oct 18, 2004...11:43AM]

> *Waste of sperm and egg—and not good ones to*
> *begin with. Worthless, lazy, self-absorbed, LOSER.*
> [oct 18, 2004 11:48AM]

You DESERVE to be with a pudgy satanic prostitute. For you, that's 'social climbing.' Scum.,, [oct 18, 2004…11:53AM]

Hope your shrink makes you feel human…asshole. [oct 18, 2004…12:56PM]

You're worthless. Go fuck another chunky lass. It's all you're good for. And barely… [oct 18, 2004…3:35PM]

Busy fucking a fat, ugly, 1 step from homeless prostitute AGAIN? Loser… [oct 18, 2004…5:30PM]

Wolfgang gets neutered tomorrow…skumbag…[oct 18, 2004…6:07PM]

So, r u ok? [oct 20, 2004…2:02AM]

nigger, fatty, whore, satanist, stripper, coke addict…what's next? I'm embarrassed ALREADY [oct 20, 2004…10:44PM]

pig. what's next? [oct 20, 2004…11:55PM]

Too much of a pansy to respond to a text? Youre worse off than i thought you were. Hope your shrink can help you—NOT be a freak. [oct 21, 2004…1:06AM]

Bedwetta's mom emailed me to apologize for her daughter's

behavior, adding that her girl had "gone a bit loopy over the past few days" and attaching an email where Bedwetta denied throwing a tantrum and kicking her mom after I'd left.

I emailed her mom back and said that it was all probably for the best. All I'd done since leaving Bedwetta was to *respond* in a conciliatory manner to messages she and her mom had sent me.

But reality hath no bearing on a woman with fake breasts scorned. Bedwetta shot me the following email:

> **Date:** *Sat, 23 Oct 2004 00:52:14*
> **Subject:** *Harassment…*
> *Jim,*
>
> *If you EVER do anything more, to make me feel REMOTELY uncomfortable – you will be sorry.*
>
> *I mean ANYWHERE and EVER.*
>
> *Cease talking about, and lying about me.*
> *Quit calling me and e-mailing my mother.*
> *Quit calling me, I would call you if I wanted to.*
> *Please, don't force me to get a restraining order.*
> *(You know, with your history…)*

Again, I had sent her a grand total of *one* text message—a gentle reply—while stoically enduring a slew of insults. And I had sent her mom merely *one* email message, responding to her mom's apology for Bedwetta's behavior. I had not attempted to call her or her mother. I was not initiating contact, only responding to it. But Bedwetta was using my "history" to concoct a fraudulent narrative where *I* was the one harassing her and her mom.

It's hard out here for an ex-con, no matter how well you behave.

Regarding Anne Lyin', the stalker who made me a convict, the last I heard of her existence was around 2009, after a woman named Anita published a mostly positive review of *Shit Magnet* online.

Anita tells me that shortly after the review went live, she started receiving multiple emails whose IP addresses all traced back to the Sacramento, CA area. She has deleted the emails, but she said they were sent from an address containing the text string "alwaysbeencrazy," which I'd known Anne to use as an email handle in the past. It was a nod to a Waylon Jennings song where he says that being crazy helped him from going insane.

According to Anita:

> *The messages consisted of repeated versions of Anne is dead, I was speaking ill of the dead and needed to remove all references to her, she was abused and I should feel bad, and God will punish me.*

That was in 2009, and it was the last evidence I'd heard that Anne Lyin', the stalker who put me in prison, even exists anymore. She was consistently loud and vocal online for the first few years after my release. Since she was the most unabashed attention whore I've ever known—she seemed to be already phoning local newspapers and magazines while still in the emergency room—I find it grossly implausible that she'd maintain her silence in an era of ubiquitous social-media platforms.

I think she's either dead, in prison, in an asylum, or so crippled with self-loathing that she's gone into self-imposed exile. If I had to choose, let her be dead—for her sake and everyone else's.

9

The Public Meltdown of a Sadomasochist

Apart from being surrounded day and night by loud smelly recidivist numskulls, the worst thing about prison was how humiliatingly dependent it made me on the outside world. I earned $48 a month working in the Oregon State Penitentiary kitchen—the maximum salary allowable by law—so if I wanted to keep myself flush in shampoo, toothpaste, coffee, notepads, and stamped envelopes, I had to ask friends on the outside to put money on my books. If I wanted to talk to anyone who wasn't a convict, I had to make $30 collect calls to friends and family members. I found it infantilizing, but having no contact with the outside world would likely have swept away the remaining scraps of my sanity like a rusty rake clawing at dry autumn leaves. So I sought solace from people who were "on the outs" however I could find it.

One of my main problems is that I have no problem accepting freaks. And at that low point in my life, I'd pretty much accept anyone who'd accept me.

Back in 1994, shortly after the "Rape Issue" of my magazine *ANSWER Me!* was released, a zinester associate named Jeff forwarded me an email he'd received from a girl named Donut. She was obsessed with serial killers, particularly Jeffrey Dahmer. She even appeared on *The Jerry Springer Show* to lay bare her obsession for the whole nation to see. In her email she told Jeff that when she saw the Rape Issue, it scared her so much that she bought a knife to protect herself.

Jeff had met Donut once in Manhattan, where she'd flown in to hook up with a man she'd met on the Internet. Jeff said Donut was "a stout woman…milkfed, as they say." She told him she had come from out West so her new online "lover" could beat her up in a hotel room. Jeff says when he met Donut, an entire side of her face was covered in bruises, yet she shrugged it all off as if it were a mere fashion choice, a quirky alternative lifestyle. As hazardous as it was, that was her kink, and she was quite candid about it. Blasé, even.

Years later when Jeff was editor for the *New York Press*, he published a cover story Donut had written about her alarming obsession:

> *Sometime this summer, in a high-rise condo look-*
> *ing out over the city, I will be given something I've*
> *been wanting for a long time: a black eye….There*
> *is no logical reason for wanting a black eye….The*
> *craving came to me last summer. Where do you*
> *search for such a thing in this day and age? The*
> *internet, of course.*

Early in 2000, I started receiving letters in prison from a girl named Donut, and after a little bit of back-and-forth it became clear that she was the same Donut who liked to meet strangers online who'd batter her until she howled for mercy. She had dropped her maiden name and married a small, shy,

Elton John-looking man who worked at Microsoft outside Seattle.

While major magazines and newspapers had covered my criminal case, I had been sitting in cages for two years without a chance to correct some egregious misinformation that had been circulating. Donut offered to start a website for me and began making weekly visits to me at the pen in Salem, OR, a 250-mile slog each way from her home in Washington.

Donut immediately began sharing the most intimate details of her highly atypical marriage with me. She said her husband was her best friend—they'd roll around on the floor wrestling and giggling and farting on one another—but she had almost no sexual desire for him. She said he wouldn't even touch her pussy unless he was wearing a rubber glove. She claimed he'd get aroused when she'd buy him bras and compliment him on his wonderful "tits." She said he knew about all her trysts in motel rooms where she'd kneel and blow guys in return for having them bash in her face. She said he'd cry his eyes out about it and begged her to stop, yet she kept doing it *and* sharing details with him about it.

When Donut started writing to me, she had been acting as an ersatz press agent and Web designer for Jason Moss, a psychology grad who'd written a best-selling book about his correspondences with serial killers.

From a letter she sent to me in prison:

> *I know it might have been Jason trying to help me, but the whole time it felt like he was trying to rip my life apart. The hardest part was that he was so aggressive and controlling and that appealed to*

me sexually, but scared me too. He took advantage
of me, talked me into buying him presents all the
time, at one time he told me he wouldn't talk to
me anymore if I didn't give him $10,000. He bad-
gered me until I sent him revealing photos, on and
on. I was a total mental wreck by the time I told
anyone what was going on.

She enclosed a printout of an email she'd sent to Jason detail-
ing her recent encounter with another faceless abuser in a
dark motel room:

I was unable to sit or stand up straight for three
days, the bruises stayed for about a month. My ass
still hurts, if you can believe, if I touch it in the
right place. The rods this guy used was tanta-
mount to using a baseball bat on my ass. It
destroyed the muscle. It was a nightmare. I'd find
myself in the shower, with the water running
down my back, and hurting my ass so bad I'd have
flashbacks and be saying "please god help me,
please god help me" over and over.

Jason's response:

I want you to see that guy A LOT more—he is
really good for you. I am happy that he treated
you in the proper way and made you feel the way

you deserved to feel. Make sure and meet with
him again!!! He is the best thing for you.

I wondered whether Donut expected me to be as cruel to her as Jason was. I also wondered if she'd be disappointed when it turned out that I wasn't.

It was about six months before I was due to be released. I explained to her that life would be rough for me when I got out and I wouldn't have much money, but I hoped I could at least partially return her kindness by talking with her about her toxic masochism. I said that unless she kept it in check, it would end disastrously for her. I told her that Jason was obviously using her and that although I appreciated her help tremendously, I'd never ask her for anything. Despite my reputation, I wasn't going to use or abuse her. For the time being, she sounded grateful about that.

Jason Moss eventually became a Las Vegas attorney. One day in 2006 he blew out his own brains.

Excerpts from letters Donut sent to me while I was in prison:

First, I know I don't "know" you but I know your
writing, your style and I actually do understand
and appreciate your views and the way you
express yourself. I enjoy it, truly, don't doubt it.
And I can empathize.

You asked why I wanted you to like me. I think it's
because I admire what you do so much and how
you do it.

I like the way you think, you are a brilliant writer and it's so NICE to have a voice out there. Technically it's not my voice, but really Jim, it is. You are the voice of a lot of people who feel just like you do. I admire what you do, and I think you are really great. And yeah, I want you to like me.

I can't do what you do. I will never write as well as you. I know this. But I can and will help any way I can to keep your voice out there. By doing the site, I'm just doing my part. I believe that I have the power, and an obligation to you to do your site. You stuck your neck out for all of us. You really did. And I'd do the same for you. I'm not doing your site out of pity, or because I think you're cute or I want you to beat me or because you're a "name." I'm doing it honestly because you deserve it, you have been through hell and you deserve someone to work hard for you like you worked hard for us.

You will hate this comparison, but I used to feel so good knowing Kurt Cobain was on this same earth with me, like, maybe life didn't suck too badly. And I always felt the same thing about you, since the first time I read your work. And I know you get shit for being you. I know that's why they put you away. It's always that way—the nail that sticks out gets hammered down, but someone has

*to be that nail. I'm like that in small ways, and
you're like that in big ways.*

*I just wanted to tell you, you're a real hero to some
people. Me.*

*I think about sex too much. I do it too much. I
don't know why. I even thought about being the
first girl to blow you after you got out of prison. I
don't know why I'd want to fuck things up like that
or what makes me think you'd want me. I'm a
dumb bitch I guess.*

*I don't know why but I wanted to show you I was
a fuck-up too, so you wouldn't feel so bad about
your situation.*

By her own estimation, Donut spent roughly 500 hours typing
up my handwritten letters and posting them to jimgoad.com.
She says she spent over $3,000 taking my collect calls. And
the day I got out of prison, she gave me $2,000 in cash so I
could find myself a place to live and avoid the dingy homeless
shelters and tuberculosis-addled halfway houses. I didn't ask
her for any of this—she offered it all. And all along the way I
thanked her, even though I suspect that most if not all of this
strange bored housewife's money came from her husband.

Over the next few years I hung out with Donut several
times in both Portland and Seattle. I took her to my favorite
bars, introduced her to a famous comedian friend of mine,
never asked her for any more help, and kept in contact with-

out the slightest of arguments. She never asked me to pay back any of the money she'd given me, although I made small gestures such as giving her signed copies of my out-of-print books to sell online.

About three years after I got out of prison, I started a message board on jimgoad.com that I called the Netjerk Lounge. Still wary from having to shut down the Yahoo! group after Anne had crashed it, I made the forum invitation-only, keeping it confined to people I thought had a sense of humor and a knack for writing. Donut was not among them.

About two years later came a nasty email from Donut saying that she knew I'd just been using her, that I never considered her a friend, that she hated all the assholes on my message board, and that even so, it was inconsiderate that I never invited her to post there.

So I made her a member. There I was again, trying to be nice.

Almost immediately she began insulting the other members, which would have been fine if she had a gift for invective or a flair for turning a phrase, but this was more like a 300-pound party-crasher wiping her ass all over the furniture. That's the main problem with open forums–it only takes one clueless boob to ruin them.

Then one day—without even realizing Donut was fat, since she used an avatar of a slim attractive blonde girl with a black eye—one of the other Lounge members, a physician, started a thread called "Fat America."

Donut got defensive. VERY defensive. Imagine 300 pounds of defensiveness.

The board had a lot of lurkers, among them some creep

who claimed to be from Colorado who never told me his name but was constantly emailing me condescending lectures about my lack of character and general failure as a human being. He also started emailing Donut, harassing her about being fat.

Things escalated on the Lounge between Donut and the other members, with Donut insisting that they didn't have a problem with her until they learned she was fat, and with them insisting that the problem wasn't her weight, it was her personality. The whole time I maintained neutrality and did not insult or taunt Donut, yet she acted certain I had set her up for public humiliation.

In truth, the only person who seemed to have a problem with Donut's weight was Donut. Her girth seemed almost like an emotional cushion, because even if she became so lean and taut that you could bounce marbles off her tummy, she'd still have the same personality. If she could blame it all on her belly, she didn't have to blame it on her soul.

In a sudden snit, Donut yanked the plug on jimgoad.com and said she'd give the site back to me if I erased everything about her that had been posted.

Scouring through old Usenet groups from the 90s revealed that Donut had left quite the electronic skid mark of erratic, hostile, and threatening behavior. Highlights of her old comments:

> *Nobody EVER wins but me. You'll learn that in*
> *time....[The Internet] keeps these messages alive,*
> *and in 10-20 years your nasty little hate-filled*
> *notes are going bite you in the ass, and with any*

*luck, permanently damage your lives forever…I'm
prepared…are you?…*Everything* is fair in love
and war…Any dirt you have on me, dearest, I
have 1/2 ton more of it on you…*

Just getting out of bed in the morning, she has a half-ton more
on EVERYONE!

Despite her belly-thumping boasts in the mid-90s about
how the Internet never forgets, here she was in 2005, suddenly
demanding that I stop "talking shit" and telling "blatant lies"
about her "over and over," although she failed to specify even
one instance of me telling an itsy-bitsy white lie about her. She
demanded that I erase all 300 pounds of her from my site.

I refused, amused that someone who with nauseatingly
sadistic glee relished the idea that someone *else's* words could
come back to haunt them on the Internet is the SAME PER-
SON who demanded I delete all *her* comments.

She sent me this:

Sent: *Sunday, April 24, 2005 7:58 PM*
Subject: *jimgoad.com*
*I don't know if you are on drugs or what. I told
you I have no intention of doing anything to jim-
goad.com. I've never lied to you. I don't give two
shits about you. Every one of my friends thinks
you're a user and loser. I always defended you, but
thanks for proving me wrong.*

*I think you're an asshole and I hope you never
contact me, mention me, talk about, etc. [My hus-*

*band] is disgusted with you, and as you know, he's
the nicest guy on earth. He things you're a piece of
crap for basically taking from me, never paying
me a dime back, calling me only when you need
something, and shitting me now when I did nothing to you, you fucking dimwit.*

*And always remember, this was YOUR choice. I'm
really glad you chose it, because I'm sick of your
drama.*

*You have no morals, no character, you are a liar,
and you and your friends are not funny (especially
the "comedians") and everyone is an idiot....*

*I guess you'll see I was right, and you were wrong,
when your site stays the same. I have friends, I
have lovers, I have school, I'm improving my life, I
don't have time for your petty, low-IQ, bullshit
games.*

Fuck off,
Donut

OK, then. Well, don't break the doorframe with your ass on
the way out.

At the time, Donut was in her mid-30s and had started
going to law school, presumably at her husband's expense. She
had been doing volunteer work at the King County, WA, pros-
ecutor's office, counseling domestic-violence victims, all while
leaving posts such as this on my forum:

*About a month ago my Adonis-like lover, my
"Michelangelo's David"-esqe lover, put this thing
around my neck that when pumped with air cuts off
your air supply, and thus I passed out. This was after
he beat the shit out of me and before I spent four hours
blowing him while wearing headphones listening to
the screams of girls being tortured.*

I posted on my board how ironic, creepy, and possibly dangerous it was that this violence-craving super-chub/super-sub who sought out men to pulverize her face was counseling domestic-violence victims.

Seemingly within minutes, Donut changed jimgoad.com's registration information:

Admin Name: *Loser Goad*
Admin Organization: *I lost to Donut*
Admin Street: *111 Loser Street*
Admin City: *ILOST*

If she's a winner, I'm happy to lose.

Maybe she turned against me because I'd been far too nice to her. When a masochist wants you to hurt them and you refuse, they can turn sadistic.

10

Ding-Dong, the Evil Satanic Wizard Is Dead

Despite its gloriously chaste mountains and its smiling virgin green trees, Oregon was my personal Bermuda Triangle. The decade I spent there would have killed 100 weaker men, 1,000 average women, ten tantrum-throwing infants, or one unicycle-riding Portland hipster with a pierced scrotum and aboriginal bones through his nose. After the obscenity trial, White House shooting, triple suicide, cancer, divorce, imprisonment, bloodshed, and unremitting chaos in the Beaver State, I packed up a truck in May of 2005 and motored back East.

In my rearview mirror I left behind the brain-damaged skinheads and lunatic exes and malevolent District Attorney and smarmy reporters and bearded throngs of lesbian lumberjack activists, moving instead to the tranquil meadows and cobblestone streets of rural Pennsylvania, where a female friend and I planned to write a book about NASCAR that never quite crept past the starting line.

While I was still in Portland, I started getting emails from a self-described fan who wasted no time in getting weird with me.

Date: *Tue, 14 Dec 2004 12:10:44 EST*

Subject: My Paranoia Concerning You
Greetings Mr. Goad: At first you seemed to be
mocking me, then what you wrote began to seem
more opaque and cryptic, and now I have come to
the (maybe utterly cock-eyed) conclusion that
what you wrote wasn't diabolically concocted by a
sinister mastermind plotting to cruelly destroy me.
Or maybe it was.

Schizophrenically Yours,
Anus Large

I had never met this odd fellow and never would. I would never so much as *speak* with him. It would be years until I even saw a picture of him, but if you can picture Yoda from *Star Wars* anally impregnating Doctor Bombay from *Bewitched*, and then the baby grew up to become a priest in the Church of Satan who belonged to several secret societies devoted to medieval swordsmanship, you're getting close.

The wizard's subsequent blizzard of fawning emails—and they kept coming, whether I responded or not—were constantly interlaced with little passive-aggressive jabs at me. If he was congratulating me for what he thought was an eminently witty post, he'd add that it was the first good one he'd seen from me in a while. He'd accuse me of having too much white guilt and of "wimping out" about racial matters, all while requesting complete anonymity if I were to post any of his racially tinged statements on my board. He scolded me for the way I ran the Lounge, which was likely his girlish way of pouting that he was never invited to join.

In a moment of indiscretion I let it slip to him that I'd gone to an emergency room for a toothache that was so bad it felt as if I was being strangled. When a doctor measured my blood pressure it was through the roof, and the doc grimly warned me that I'd probably have a stroke if it weren't brought under control.

The next day, my friend Vladimir emailed me Russian folk remedies for high blood pressure. Anus Large had told him. It felt like digital bad-touching that Mr. Large would grab this little acorn of health information and run blabbing like an eager squirrel about it to anyone who'd listen.

I asked Large why he was sharing my medical info with others. He apologized, then confronted me about something that had been plaguing his beleaguered soul. He wanted to know if during a recent trip through Atlanta I'd "talked shit" about him to my friend Nick's girlfriend Sandy, because he said Sandy was acting standoffishly toward him ever since my visit.

This struck me as queer, because I'd never even mentally placed Large in the Atlanta area. To me, he only existed in cyberspace. It probably would have broken his meth-punctured heart to know I wasn't thinking of him *at all* while in Georgia, much less "talking shit" about him.

I called up Nick and asked him what he knew about Anus Large.

Large had hung out with Nick for a short spell, but the corpulent, sweaty pig-worm vomited on Nick in a moving vehicle, preyed upon Nick's natural generosity, gave away, lost, or sold the items that Nick spent time and effort creating for him at no charge, demanded more from Nick, and then spun preposterously delusional tales that Nick owed him money because of it. Nick wisely decided to close the vault on him.

Nick explained that Anus was a Hep C-positive soul-sucking leech who was on death's door due not only to a rotting liver, but also because he kept guzzling hard liquor and imbibing baseball-sized rocks of crystal meth against his doctor's orders. He told me he'd take care of it and sent Anus this email:

> *Anus,*
>
> *Seriously, I've asked you time and again to leave me out of all the crazy ass crank letters you incessantly send around the horn, but you insist on embarrassing me to no end....Jim Goad just gave me one of those now familiar "What's the deal with this Large guy?" calls and said you sent some long goofy rant about Sandy not liking you, etc., etc....You really do have way too much time on your hands or perhaps your drinking or recent lack of has caused an imbalance that's prompting titanic new fears and delusions to take root...whatever the situation, get it fixed and kindly leave me and mine totally out of your future correspondence to others....I've never had to deal with so much nationwide childish horseshit in my life and every bit of it hails from you alone. With your constant bungling and interloping, you've single-handedly done more to create grief for me than any of my sworn enemies...Is that your intention? It appears so, since I've asked*

*many times now that you leave me out of your
psycho-cyberdramas and nutty networking.*

Nick

Anus sent me a one-line pleading:

What did I ever do to deserve this, Jim?

I replied:

*1. You send me a weird, cryptic email asking
whether I'd planted evil seeds in a certain girl's
brain regarding you.*

2. You reveal this girl to be Sandy.

*3. I call up Nick and ask him what's up with this
guy who thinks I'd talk shit about him to Sandy.*

*4. You wonder what you ever could have done to
deserve such treatment at my hands.*

Is this what you're saying?

He countered:

*Well, actually now that you put it so concisely, yes!
Apparently, my earlier accusation was quite accu-
rate. Snitch!*

What did I "snitch" about? That he was weird?

That was in June 2006, and that's all it took. I didn't need to know anything else about him. He had "weirded" himself out of my life. I never contacted him again.

But alas and alack, he had only yet *begun* to contact me. Over the next four years he would proceed to send me—and seemingly everyone in my periphery—messages that lurched back and forth between belligerence, apologies, and flaming hostility again when I'd ignore his apology. Through it all, I did not respond. He was barking at a wall of silence. For FOUR YEARS.

I moved down to Florida in late 2006 to stay with my brother while I finished writing and designing my fourth book, *Jim Goad's GIGANTIC BOOK OF SEX*. Cruising MySpace, I began corresponding with a girl in Atlanta who knew both Nick and Large. They'd all attended a wedding together, but when Large tried to give her a goodnight smooch, she turned away and hopped out of his car. The first time she and I ever spoke on the phone, we talked about how strange he was.

I moved up to Atlanta in early 2007 and began dating the girl, whom I would marry a year later. When Large found out we were together, he warned her that I was not only a woman-beater who would immediately begin punching her in the face, I was also a puritanical teetotaler who would be no fun for her at all—at least not as much fun as a swingin' cat such as Large, who gets so fucked-up that he pukes his Hep C-laden vomit in your face while you're driving.

Over the next few years he repeatedly contacted her to explain that he knew she was an innately good person and therefore would take his "side" in this matter once he was able to, you know, thoroughly explain his side to her.

By this time, I didn't need to hear his "side." His behavior told me all I needed to know about him. He could present his case like William Jennings Bryan, and I'd still think he was a jerkoff.

My wife sent him an admirably restrained email stating that we really don't spend much time thinking about him and that he needed to find something else to do with his life besides harass and insult—and then try to make nice with—people who'd ceased all contact with him.

Nope. The messages continued. In one direction. From him to us. While trying to make amends, he bleated on and on about his "illness" and "disability" in a repugnantly effeminate dungheap of self-pity. When I'd ignore him yet again, his mood would turn foul once more.

What a mess of contradiction this obese warthog turned out to be!

He was a proud white supremacist who lived on welfare in his mother's basement.

He was a self-declared full-blown heterosexual that no woman on Earth would want.

He was a self-appointed master aesthete who had never created a single artifact that anyone in the solar system desires or collects.

He was a supernaturally powerful satanist and warlock who likely had trouble passing a solid bowel movement or achieving a simple erection without massive pharmaceutical intervention.

The harassing emails, which had started in the summer of

2006, continued throughout 2007. Late that year I became editor of a website called Consumption Junction. Almost immediately a nasty little mole popped up in the comment section calling himself "Decster" but whose grandiloquent prose style and endless besmirchment of me made clear it was Anus Large.

It was around this time that I'd announced I was going to become a father. Decster, who openly speculated that I may be Jewish due to my ample proboscis, openly delighted in the idea that my infant spawn would come down with Tay-Sachs disease and die from it.

Wishing death upon my baby, are we? All righty, then, sir. I chose a screen name that signified I knew his identity and left the following message under his:

> *Go die of Hep-C in your mother's basement, you*
> *fat, worthless creep.*

As the urban youth are fond of saying, this is what took it to that next level. Fueled by this insult and outraged that he'd been unmasked, Large began seeking vengeance almost immediately. He sent the following messages to my friend Lorin, who passed them along to me:

> **Date:** *Nov 16, 2007 7:20 PM*
> **Subject:** *Greetings Lorin*
> *Someone is mentioning my Hepatitis C on your*
> *most recent edirorial,and they have figured out*
> *who I am. I suspect that it isn't you,Lou,but I*
> *think you might know who this sissy is. Please tell*

*them that I'm ready to meet then face to face,and
sttle this onvce and for all. They're right,with my
severely damaged heart and advanced Hepatitis,I
haven't got much longer to live. Byt I'd be anxious
to give it a go hand to hand,and show this eunuch
who is the better man. And,my compliments
regarding your writing were sincere. What reason
could I possibly have to play the sycophant? Don't
mistakke kindness for weakness Lorin! Don't
mean to sound harsh,but I know you are a
staunch admirer of a fellow that I used to admire
myself,and can sort of understand why you'd
acceept his opinions about anyione because of his
notoriety and illustrious friends. But he slanders
me egregiously,and I regret that the truth might be
a bitter pill to swallow. I find explaining myself
partucularly onerous.so I'm gonna stop. But I will
be more that happy to fill you in on anything
you'd like to have thje truth about…I appreciated
the "War Is Groovy"schtick,the "Be Mean to Girls
day"and especially the Don Nazi moniker you
once answered to. I only seek to wise you up,little
brother. I had labored under the delusion that I
wAs doing you a favor by introducing that Jen
stripper/synth player girl to Bougas … he sure as
hell appreciated the gesture. I reckoned that you
and I were square;maybe we are! But I have to
know who gave out my initials and medical status.
This fucker is mine! Put 'em in touch with me,and
I'll owe you BIG TIME!*

Kindest Regards, Anus Large p.s. You aren't partivculaly averse to a bit of entertaining unpleasantness,are you my fine lad? I want this fucker;if you don'y care for me,maybe if you're lucky,I'll be exterminated! On the othet hand,I'll give the schmuck a bit of wisdom to ruminate over. Win Win situation,eh? Fun for all!

Date: *Nov 17, 2007 3:47 PM*
Subject: *RE: Greetings Lorin*
Someone said "I know who you are DB/and I hope you die of your hepatitis in your Mother's basement,you fat useless fuck."I didn't measn to inply that you sent the message/because you obviously couldn't care less about such petty shit. But I thought you might be inrerested in hazarding a guess as to the author's identity for fun. I really want to meetthisperson,and I do apologixe if this was so out of left field that it was less than pleasant to consider dealing with. It'll take unususal tactics to flush this fucker out,and I don't have unlimited time available to me,I regret to say. Your kind patience with a seeming maniac such as myself is aboveand beyond the call of duty,Lorin,and is rather touching.*This coward that doesn't know me personally ,(otherthanmy name and life-threatening health conditions)and wishes me a rapid demise is someone whose identity is of great interest to me. Sorry to bother you,but I don't expect you be a

*snitch.ifyouknowwho it is,give'em my contact info/
and see whethertheyhave the balls to fuck with
me/damaged heart or no damaged heart! *That
was not intended to be sarcastic/but sincere.*

At first he seemed to think the culprit behind the "Go die"
message was Nick, so he started threatening to expose sensitive information about Nick in some dim quest to bring him
down and pay him back for whatever imaginary indignities
he'd convinced himself Nick had foisted upon him.

Date: *Nov 19, 2007 11:33 AM*
Subject: *RE: Greetings Lorin*
*The slander i referred to in my last missive bears
all of the earmarks of the work of Bougas. I have
very little respect for that wretched auTOGRAPH
COLLECTOR,MAINL Y BECAUSE HE FALSELY
ACCUSED ME OF BETRAYING HIM. I HAVE
NEVER DONE ANY SUCH THING/BUT I
COULD DESTROY HIM IF I WERE TO CEASE
TO CONTINUE TO WITHHOLD THE BIG-
TIME MUD I HAVE REFRAINED FROM
UNLEASHING. iF HE WANTS A PHYSICAAL
CONFRONTATION/HE ONLY LIVES 30 MILES
AWAY/AND I'D BE HAPPY TO PUT AN END
TO HIS LIES! i know that you respect him,thus
my decision to involve you in this unpleasantness.
After all the threatening message was left on your
hobosexual editorial. I intend to explore every
possible lead I have on this,Lorin. I am fucking*

furious. Ithe last thing I intended to do was to upset you/because you have been the soul of civility,even when I might've been somewhat offensive. Fron what little info I possess with regard to you,I would judge you as a decent sort. If you choose to ignore this,I think you know what my next tactic will have to be. With regret that I was forced to bother you with this umpleasantness,cordially, Anus Large.

And then, after all his leads dried up, he rightly concluded that I had left the message. He came to me in peace, seeking only to "avoid any ugly displays":

Date: *Wed, 23 Jan 2008 19:48:25 -0500*
Subject: *Clearing up a misunderstanding once and for all…*
Greetings Jim, This is Anus Large, and I have come to the conclusion that it's time to offer a possible tentative olive branch. We do live in the same town, so perhaps it would behoove us both to reconsider each other's take on this unfortunate and somewhat ill considered position.…If it becomes apparent that I'm wasting my time attempting to defend my position, I'll just let it go.…In light of the fact that you are a father-to-be, and your main squeeze is a young lady whom I discern as having very good qualities, and very good for you ,if we were to unexpectedly encounter one another, I'd like to avoid any ugly

*displays....On a more somber note, I wasn't
exactly enthralled with the "Decster is Anus
Large", and the low blow of "Why don't you die of
hepatitis in your Mom's basement?". It obviously
was you....I'm willing to let bygones be bygone but
it all hinges on your willingness to listen with an
open mind to the revelations I could impart. In
any event, congrats on your incipient blessed
event.*

I ignored him again. Two days later his stomach had soured:

Date: *January 25, 2008 8:37:54 PM EST*
Subject: *The passing of my magnanimous
mood...*
leads me to withdraw my earlier generous offer.

One sunny morning in June of 2008, I had a *grand mal* seizure
and was rushed to a hospital, where an MRI revealed a plum-
sized benign brain tumor. Over a nine-hour operation they
sawed open my skull and plucked out most of the offending
mass. I had another massive seizure right after the operation.

Large hopped merrily onto my wife's MySpace page, gloating about how "hilarious" my brain tumor was and how his
demonic powers had caused it. He also sent her a message in
French that when translated read, "You will have many more
troubles."

Date: *Jun 25, 2008 8:16 AM*

Subject: *My Inevitable Righteous Vengeance Against My Enemies …*

If ANYONE has a problem with my gloating over the misfortune of a certain cowardly woman-beating enemy of mine who openly called for my death on a public message board(and whom I called out for a physical confrontation, at 52, after 3 heart attacks and hep-C … seems I -don't have a vagina, so he won't fight hand to hand)…WHOMEVER you may be, first of all,keep in mind that his punishment cured him,and even saved his life,and second of all,if your loyalty to me is that flimsy,GO FUCK YOURSELF! If you love me,celebrate my victories with me! If you don't,I sever all ties with you! Certain rare exceptions may be made,as I see fit.

Love, Anus

She again asked him to stop. He didn't. Legally, when you tell someone to leave you alone and they keep contacting you, it's harassment. In Georgia, one infraction is a misdemeanor. Two is a felony. He was already in the multiple-felony zone.

With two felonies on *my* record and facing an opponent with a fatal blood-borne pathogen coursing through his veins, stomping his face into the concrete and snapping his neck with my hands wasn't the most desirable option.

But it was time to hit at least *somebody* back. So my wife called the cops on him. When a detective contacted him,

Large immediately tried to explain his "side," but the detective told him to zip his mouth and leave us alone.

Which he did. For nearly two years. Until…

Date: *Thursday, April 22, 2010 12:36:34 AM*
Subject: *I'm not going to insult you,but compliment you…fear not. No cops,okay?*
… Jim, I never would have attacked you so cruelly if you hadn't told me to DIE…I was in a particularly hostile mood, exacerbated by my abnormally high serum ammonia levels…that never fails when it comes to inspiring one to vicious behavior.…You are sort of in my town,you know,and I'd prefer to avoid any unpleasantness that might arise if we encounter each other at one place or another, I no longer harbor any enmity toward you.…I have proffered the olive branch. The ball is in your court, sir. Best to thee and thine, Anus Large p.s. neither do I expect that we'll become fast friends…I appreciate your honest take on things,but I'm no suck-up to the famous and quasi-famous…I've got my own schtick.

Schtick it up your ass. Schtick it DEEP up your ass along with every one of your olive branches and fig leaves.

Again my wife called the police. Large told the detective he would cease his harassment if we would stop making "slanderous" comments about him, even though we weren't making *any* comments about him, and the cop told him to shut his piehole. He finally left us alone.

He picked up the slack by sending unsolicited emails trying to explain his "side" of the matter to EVERYONE on my message board, but since he had not a droplet of natural charm in his fat-clogged frame, he failed in every case. So then he got nasty with each one of *them*, too, accusing them of being helplessly devoted and brainwashed members of the Goad Cult.

He sent this to a friend of mine who calls himself Shift:

> **Date:** *May 17, 2010 2:03:52 PM PDT*
> **Subject:** *Forgiveness?*
> *Maybe I should forgive you for the scurrilous reply you sent to my friendly e-mail of several months ago, as I realize that you have to be suffering more than a little brain damage from having your schnozz crammed up dickhead's lower GI tract for so long, cunt.*

To Shaun Partridge, another member of my Lounge, he emailed a prognostication that "The Partridge will die in May."

In early 2013, the portly annelid made a fittingly shameful final bow. He traveled alone (naturally) to attend a revival screening of a Vincent Price horror film and as he sat ogling the screen, his ravaged organs suddenly began shutting down. His instinctual reaction to feeling his life force ebb was to abandon the family car, hail a taxi, and promptly scurry back to his mommy's protective shell far across town. Large arrived at the homestead just in time to enter the front door and blurt out to his mom that she needed to pay his cab fare. Then he flopped dead of heart failure on his mother's living-room floor, rather than of Hep C in her basement as I'd wished.

The next day his family sent out a frantic online message stating they needed help finding the family vehicle, as they had no idea where Anus had left it. He was a pain the ass to his facilitators, like he had been to everyone else, right up to the end. I believe he may be the first person in world history to die from a bad personality.

11

Happy Tumor-Breeding!

The year 2008 was trauma-packed even by *my* standards. In addition to my brain surgery, my wife got infected with the potentially fatal MRSA virus at the hospital in the course of delivering our son; she was robbed at gunpoint a week after Obama was elected president; and my car was T-boned and totaled by an uninsured driver over the Thanksgiving holiday, spraying glass into the back seat and all over my four-month-old baby boy.

Ever since I left prison in late 2000, I'd done freelance writing, editing, and design for a free Portland sex-industry magazine. I was set up with the job—employment was a condition of my parole—less than two weeks out of the joint by the magazine's original owner Frank Faillace, a gentle soul and a prince among men. Not only did he create a position for me that he didn't really need to fill, he also negotiated the puppy-hostage crisis with Methrissa and returned the young pre-teen pug to me after a tense weeklong standoff.

Frank eventually sold the magazine and focused on managing Portland nightclubs, bequeathing the mag's legacy to a new owner and ad salesman. They were more the caliber of dudes you'd expect to receive self-esteem boosts by being involved in any way with a free sex-industry rag.

The new owner was **Cryan Baby**, the mag's former sales

manager. He was born in Italy under a different name and came to America under circumstances I still don't quite comprehend. From my experience, he tended to emulate a pimp's approach to managing his independent contractors—it didn't even matter if you performed well as long as you desperately needed the job. For reasons that are still unclear to me, Cryan seemed to be under the impression that he was a black man.

The ad guy was named John, and I dubbed him "**Jon Bon Voji**" in homage to his 1980s hair-band desert-reptile aesthetic. He was such a rocker, I don't believe he would be able to stop rockin' even if forced at gunpoint. He was the "brains" behind Portland's annual "Ink-N-Pink" competition, a tasteful pageant of the Rose City's finest tattooed strippers splaying their vulvas onstage in the quest to seize the coveted crown of "Miss Ink-N-Pink."

John and the magazine had a previous falling out a few years earlier, and I entered the fray by writing several mocking articles about him. I also circulated a naked photo of him he'd stupidly left on an office computer that showed him pensively staring off-camera while displaying a male organ whose size invited ridicule.

Jon Bon Voji was infuriating to work with because he was, I will remind you again, the kind of guy who wasn't ashamed to be working for a free sex-industry rag. In fact, it may have been his life's central accomplishment.

Less than a month after my brain surgery I was back working full-time during the day at a square job for a medical company, and thus my porno-mag freelance work got packed into three or four all-nighters every month. And every month John would manage to find a way to fuck up my schedule and make me wait hours for him to get it together. He'd do things such as keep me hanging all night waiting for an article he'd promised to deliver, then claim the next morning that he'd left it in his backpack at a nightclub the fire department had raided. It was the sex-industry-dude equivalent of "The dog ate my homework" month after month, year after year.

During magazine deadline in July 2008, a mere month after my brain surgery, we got into an argument via Yahoo! Instant Messenger about how to lay out an article written by some Seattle heavy-metal guitarist.

Cryan Baby, the Italian white man who thought he was black, got dragged into the dispute. I told him my side, and John told him his side, adding that he thought my brain surgery had fucked up my mind and I wasn't making any sense and may possibly be brain-damaged.

Low blow there, *kemosabe*. That's the sort of flagrant foul that gets you thrown out of the game.

I was making enough money at my regular job that I didn't have to waste my nights waiting for some cheesy porno dude to quit playing *Guitar Hero* long enough to accuse me of being brain-damaged. This led to a text argument between Cryan and me. When I told him I was quitting, this is the last message Cryan texted me:

Happy tumor-breeding!

Thanks, homie.

In their next issue, John wrote a brilliant, Swiftian two-page article about me called "My Tumor is Bigger Than Yours." A man of intense originality, he brought up the fact that I'm an evil woman-beater. A clever man, he referred to me as "Choad" rather than Goad, which hurt my feelings and continues to hurt them. Although I'd quit, he claimed I'd been fired. He also harped on the fact that I wrote a lot about my penis for the magazine, and I can't quite blame him because I've seen his penis and understand why he'd be upset. He also saw fit to mention my newborn son. Class act, Strip Club Guy!

He also continually smeared me as a "racist" in that article, which is precious because in our fatal Instant Messaging session, he was the only one calling the magazine's only black writer a "nigger":

> **John Bon Voji:**
> *im being bitched out because he doesnt understand the nigger*
> *understand my frustration right now partner?*

More than five years later, John and Cryan are still both working at that magazine. I mention that only to gloat.

12

You're a Sociopath, So I Want to Blow Your Brains Out

I sing country music now and then mainly to confuse people, and through an odd chain of events I wound up spending the summer of 2007 touring the USA as the opening act for Hank Williams III. Prior to the tour, I received an email from a girl in Texas named **Sally Weaselly**. She invited me to hang out if I passed through the Lone Star State—a flat, awful plain of dust that is so named because even its residents only give it one star.

I ignored the email. Apparently this is a hanging offense in Texas.

Sally reemerged three years later and launched into a full-bore nitro-burnin' online Tet Offensive against me. She said she was majoring in psychology at college and had concluded through her research that I was a narcissistic sociopath who, according to the official diagnostic manuals, did not deserve custody of my son. She said that her stepfather had *also* been a narcissistic sociopath—what are the odds?—and that she intended to reclaim her sanity and pride by trying to destroy me.

Again—except for *reading* an email of hers in 2007, I'd never interacted with the girl.

One night in 2010 she left a pair of fire-breathing comments on an article I'd written for streetcarnage.com. The comments are extremely similar, but just different enough that I'll present them both. As one associate noted, this is sort of like a "Director's Cut" of what is essentially one very crazy comment:

> **Submitted on 2010/03/17 at 11:26pm**
> *You represent everything I hate about people, the world, society and life. Superiority, greed. close – minded shallowness, sexism … a bunch of shit-heads on your website worshiping a clockwork orange .. the fact that it's called Star Chamber .. The way everyone on their pathetically feels some sense of specialness and validation because they're typing on your stupid fucking website. Oh and your wife- that stupid gothic bullshit, the feeling like she is safe because she's with a fucked up sociopath to protect her. Oh , it all sounds so god-damn familiar. How many dumb bitches out there will shack up with empathy-less fuckups because it makes them feel "safe" … Oh god and referencing elizabeth bathory as her hero.. what the fuck .. god it all makes me sick to my stomach. I know true sociopathy, true pain and what real hatred feels like and mine is stronger than yours will ever fucking be. I wish I could really really meet all you losers .. I really really do. I'd like to see you try and*

*condescend to someone who's more fucked up than
you are. all those dumb bitches you dated pretending to be sociopaths and taking your hits like victims .. please .. i'd like you to meet someone who
maybe worse than you, angrier than you and see
you try that bullshit. But I'm sure you'll keep
going, keep writing these bullshit articles, keep seeing the world through a fucked up lens and die
feeling superior.*

Submitted on 2010/03/17 at 11:16pm
*The more and more I think about it, the more I
realize you represent everything I hate about
human beings, society and life in general.
Pathetic, angry, false-superiority, pride, condescending, posturing, mental illness, etc. I hate even
more the pathetic losers on your stupid fucking
website. Every time I read your twitter posts I
want to come find you and blow your brains out.
What's with all the wannabe sociopaths on that
site .. they drive me fucking crazy. The stupid
clockwork orange worshiping dickheads .. the fact
that it's called "star chamber" .. your wife's
pathetic reference to elizabeth bathory being her
hero. Yeah, you're all so fucking cool and scary ..
really .. i'd like to show you true sociopathy and
what a real shitty childhood looks like. You'll just
keep writing this stupid, trite , bullshit articles.
You'll die being the same immature sexist narcissistic prick. You'll never see anything other than*

your close-minded point of views. It all makes me sick to my fucking stomach. And the fact that these people keep publishing this bullshit .. this world is fucked up and so are you. You are everything wrong with the world. I hate you more than you will ever understand and fathom. And I know hatred and feel it stronger than you ever fucking will.

OK, then, Miss Future Psychologist. Rather than engage with another scorned psycho, I'll just banish you and your daddy issues to the Cyberian wastelands by blocking you.

Submitted on 2010/03/23 at 4:37pm
Wow. do you block everyone who disagrees with you?…Is it too harsh to realize that you're nothing but a walking, breathing personality disorder (one you admit to having online, so I didn't diagnose you). Oh and go ahead and trace my IP address. Do you think I give a fuck? Am I supposed to be afraid of you? I've already had a narcissistic boyfriend try and kill me, he didn't succeed. I've had a NPO stepfather try to destoy me, and he didn't succeed. I'm not afraid of anything. i'll give you my own address if you want it. You're not as smart and scary as you pretend to be.

As with the others, I did not respond. At some point during an 11-month span of constant shrieking buzzsaw harassment without so much as a chirp from me in response, Sally teamed up with a young ginger fella from Alabama who called himself Sardonicus, which, when you think about it, is really an evil and scary-sounding name. Sardonicus claimed to be a schizophrenic and a "true" misanthrope—as opposed to me, whom he accused of being a fake misanthrope.

So one of them wanted to kill me for being evil and the other wanted to kill me for not being evil enough? Whatever works for you kids. Sooner or later, the crazy lovebirds parted ways. It's sad—I really thought that one was going to last. But Sally kept harassing me solo again.

She tried "friending" my wife on Facebook and me on MyLife. Neither of us responded.

Using the fake identity "Nancy Snow," she sent me an email in February 2011. She'd taken the worst picture of my wife she could find, put it on hotornot.com, and was mocking the fact that the picture had received a low score. I responded to the email, being careful to refer to her in the third person because I wanted to retain my unblemished record of never having had contact with her.

> **Subject:** *Re: hey i saw slampira on hotornot i just wanted to warn you*
> **Date:** *Tue, February 15, 2011 12:50 pm*
> *Over the past year, I have compiled a trove of evidence, all of it verified through Internet Service Providers, that Sally Weaselly is a mentally unbalanced stalker who has openly threatened my life.*
>
> *Despite nothing but silence on my part, she has*

*not gone away. She has lately taken to harassing
my wife.*

*Friends and I, including lawyers and Web technol-
ogy specialists, have compiled a damning stack of
evidence regarding her mental state that will
ensure she will never be able to find employment
as a psychologist.*

"Nancy Snow" quickly emailed back, referring to Sally in the
third person:

*sally has a severe case of schizophrenia and has no
idea what she is doing. the voices tell her everything.*

She left me alone for another two months, then left me this
message on Facebook:

5/17, 10:33pm
sorry
*im sorry about what happened. the truth is i am
sensitive and pictured you and your wife sitting at
your computer laughing at me calling me a cry-
baby when in fact i havent cried in over three
years. i was filled with anger. which is dumb. this
is just the internet. the truth is, your wife is beautiful and i was just jealous because i had a crush
on you even though you probaby think i'm ridicu-
lous and an idiot. bye.*

I'm not going to say "bye" because I never even said "hi."

13

The Shunning of Anti-Semitic Steve

During my tireless, tiresome, and tiring exploits online, I've found there are two breeds of Internet cranks that are far more annoying and persistent than any other:

- Those who blame Jews for everything (AKA, "Jew Hunters" or "The Men Who Taste Jews in Their Sandwiches");
- Those who don't blame Jews for anything (AKA "Nazi Hunters" or "The Self-Appointed Stormtroopers Who Enforce Godwin's Law").

A willowy guy from the Pacific Northwest named Steve belonged to the first category. I christened him "**Anti-Semitic Steve**." He constantly bent the ears of the unwilling in his quest to prove the Hidden Jewish Hand behind global events. I don't mind the topic *per se* because I'm drawn to taboo subjects. But the topic is SO *verboten*—truly, the Holocaust is our modern version of Christ's resurrection and one can't question even the smallest detail about it without being excommunicated from society—that it tends to appeal to certain types of misfits who don't mind being huge pests about the subject whether you want to hear about it or not. They almost make you wish the Nazis had room for 6,000,001.

Steve was also like Anus "The Evil Satanic Wizard" Large in that he seemed incapable of giving me a compliment without wrapping it in an insult. Over the years he wore on my nerves and those of the Netjerks until many of them told him never to contact them again. For someone who claimed to hate Jews so much, Steve sure was pushy.

I finally told Steve to go away, and he sent back some whimpering email telling me that he harassed me so that I would stop taking myself so seriously. Like many of the other stalkers, he was on a moral mission to teach me a lesson. I countered that his behavior made it impossible for me to take *him* seriously—so again, please leave, Steve.

Shortly thereafter, Steve had set up fake accounts on MySpace and Twitter posing as me. He used a real picture of me taken at Hoover Dam as the profile picture.

I confronted Steve, who quickly relinquished the MySpace and Twitter accounts.

This was early in 2009, when Facebook was still relatively obscure, so I jumped onto Facebook and seized the "jimgoad" URL before Steve could rub his highly non-kosher ball sweat all over it.

I imagine that Steve is leading a quiet life somewhere, reading Ezra Pound near a fireplace while blaming Jews for his personality.

14

Poopy Unplugged

My experiences with Fat Donut should have taught me to beware of fans that come bearing gifts.

Although I believe that **Poopy Partridge** might consider himself an artist—he may have painted a toolshed once or twice and done some sort of lo-fi home-studio musical project involving his dog—his personality and skill set are those of a fan. A devoted fan. A fan that does you favors even if you don't request them.

Born, raised, and still living on a desolate patch of dirt in far southwestern Virginia, Poopy told me that my book *The Redneck Manifesto* was unlike anything he'd ever read before. He liked to spread his fandom around and was an even more devoted follower of Shaun Partridge, founder of the Partridge Family Temple. Shaun had been an *ANSWER Me!* contributor, member of my website's message board for several years, and a founding member of Unpop Art.

Although the Partridge Family Temple is obviously a parody of a cult, Poopy joined it with the enthusiasm of a blinkered devotee. Working as a mortician, he filmed himself placing a cassette player inside a corpse's body cavity and playing Partridge Family songs. It seemed as if he didn't mind the possibility of getting arrested so long as he could take one for the team.

Poopy melted so entirely into the team, his online screen persona incorporated "Unpop" into his first name and "Partridge" as his surname—the monikers of two overlapping scenes that he had no hand in creating but to which he surrendered every last shred of individual identity, if it can be assumed he ever had such a thing in the first place.

Poopy wanted sorely to be a team player, even if his meager talents meant he'd never qualify to be part of the starting lineup. Even when it was revealed to him that an Unpop "artist" who died of a heroin overdose had described Poopy as a creepy hanger-on, Poopy still seemed to consider himself a member of the squad rather than an overeager water boy. Since no one asked him to star in the porn movie, he volunteered for the role of a fluffer.

My pal Lorin was was one of the original Unpop artists—unlike Poopy, who was never more than an acolyte and someone who mailed out Unpop T-shirts. Lorin had a falling out with Unpop's organizer and was suddenly "popped," or "de-popped," or whatever you'd call it when you're no longer Unpop. Although to my knowledge Poopy and Lorin never had an argument, the moment Lorin was excommunicated, Poopy would act disgusted at the very mention of his name, as if Lorin was some kind of pariah heretic.

Poopy was extremely generous toward me although I'd never asked him for a thing. Often when I passed through Virginia while driving cross-country or was heading further South for NASCAR races, he'd offer to let me stay at the free house his family had given him. He once called in a favor and set me up with a free motel room. Through a friend of his, he provided me with free server space for my website for years.

He drove four hundred miles to attend my wedding reception. He drove seven hundred miles to attend the kickoff of my musical tour in 2007. He was devoted and friendly and never demanding or impolite.

The first time he got weird was in the middle of 2009 when he told me that a girl had accused him of being nothing more than an "empty online gimmick," or something to that effect.

"Well, Poopy," I wrote jokingly, "I've always known you were nothing more than an empty online gimmick, so it's cool."

He sharply asked me what the hell that was supposed to mean.

I told him to calm down, mildly rattled that he didn't realize I was joking. It was obviously a sensitive issue for him.

It all went bad at Christmas in 2009. Poopy had tried and failed to make plans to visit Shaun Partridge out in Portland, so he asked if he could come and stay at my place for a few days between Christmas and New Year's.

I diplomatically tried explaining that I'd be working that week so I wouldn't have much time to spend with him. Oh, that was OK, he said...but could he still come?

At the time I was legally forbidden to drive due to seizures I'd had after brain surgery, requiring me to trek two hours to work each way using two trains and two buses. I asked Poopy to at least pick me up from work and drive me home on the day he came down from Virginia.

Instead, he showed up unannounced at my house, scaring the hell out of my mother-in-law and requiring me to take those awful two buses and two trains home. Still, I entertained him at my house for two nights, bought him meals, and did my best to be a courteous host even though he was essentially uninvited and infringing on my work schedule.

The third day he was in Atlanta, he texted me about an hour before I got off work saying that he had to pick up some girl from where she worked and I'd have to take the buses and trains home.

It was near-freezing outside and raining. I never saw or spoke with him again.

He went back to Virginia a few days later without calling. When I checked on his Twitter feed, it was suddenly full of nasty messages directed at an unnamed foe. This was an abrupt switch from the tone of his feed prior to his visit, which had been filled with his ham-handed attempts to be clever or re-Tweets of things I'd posted. I presumed that all these nasty new messages were directed at me.

Within a few days, he emailed me to ask whether some things I'd Tweeted were directed at him. I told him to leave me the fuck alone.

Almost immediately after I cut him loose, he tried buddying up with at least three of my close friends, all of whom are semi-famous and all of whom shunned him. He tried contacting my wife once or twice, but she snubbed him, too. I reckon that when he's not performing unsolicited favors for people, this lowly Scene Leech gets snubbed a lot. That might be due to the fact that a mutual acquaintance described his personality as that of "dry toast."

But he did leave me alone—I mean, at least he never contacted me *directly* again. Yet for about a solid year thereafter, his Twitter account consisted of little more than bitter subtweets directed at someone he eventually called "Stinky

McRude." This is rich, since I can think of few things more rude than leaving your unwilling-yet-gracious host sitting alone at a bus stop in freezing rain because some scruffy Atlanta scenester gash finally answered your phone call and there was a chance that your desperate shovelface might score.

Although he only mentioned me by name once during this yearlong barrage, it seems clear he was talking about me because several of the messages came directly after things I'd posted on Twitter:

> *Jim Goad @jimgoad January 27, 2010*
> *If the snake's retarded, expect the venom to be retarded, too.*

> *Poopy 28 Jan 10*
> *nosey it up with fake screen names, stalk my sites for ideas & hack my ideas while calling me retarded. Retard, thats retarded.*

> *Jim Goad @jimgoad February 26, 2010*
> *Every time I move my bowels, I'm reminded of you.*

> *Poopy 26 Feb 10*
> *so, you're stating that when your anus has things moving out of it you're reminded of other people? Do you wish it was a priest too?*

> *Jim Goad @jimgoad February 2, 2010*
> *We have creative differences. For instance. I'm creative.Poopy 2 Feb 10*

your idea of 'creative' is very similar to a drag
queen squealing unreliable amounts of blab &
begging for the attention of young boys

Jim Goad @jimgoad March 10, 2010
Most of the time, merely having to hang out with
someone is too high a price to pay, no matter what
service was rendered.

Poopy 18 Mar 10
No one said you had to hang out, stink daddy.
Social parasites and social beggars should just
move from host to host.

He took to calling himself an "alpha male," failing to realize that an alpha male *has* followers, while a beta male *is* a follower. Crucial distinction.

Like the Evil Satanic Wizard, he also appeared under the impression that he had magical powers that could cause me harm. (Also like the Evil Satanic Wizard, he sorely lacked any magical powers that would give him *personal* charm.) When my website crashed for about nine days in March 2010, he Tweeted this:

your overt and covert workings against me are
why all of your hardware fails.

Workings? Who has the time for workings when you're working?
Other half-baked metaphysical Tweet-threats included:

*every brick wall of my Temple is grounded 7 feet
into the high ground so i can watch human
garbage like you float by in flood water*

*You're no one's friend, not one, none. You're a par-
asite & a display. Don't ever request my comfort.
Go fuck your ego so we'll have you shot.*

*I dont believe in Karma, but i cant stop the pun-
ishment youll recieve for working against
me......and its real.*

*Whats classic is your "friends" just cant bear
telling you that you deserve every, lasting bit of
trauma that fucks your life.*

*All my mistakes are premium bait for decapitating
your head from its throne.*

*You have to kill it first, because it will not stop
hunting you.*

Since he'd known me for years, he was familiar with the sagas
of several other case studies in this book, but suddenly he was
alleging that all this "stalking" was just in my head:

*When all else fails, you could always just keep
masturbating to imaginary stalkers and fans.*

Stinky McRude cries inside as his girlfriends are

*"beards" & he has to use fake screen names to
stalk his enemies for fresh ideas.*

*Mention of imaginary stalkers is the classic indi-
cator of garbage on the line.*

Other motifs involved Stinky McRude being a closeted homosexual with a small penis. Poopy also had the wisdom, class,
and grace to mention Stinky's firstborn child a couple times.

Then again, maybe *none* of this was about me, although a
lot of it *seems* to be. But that's just what a foul-smelling ego-
maniacal needle-dicked closet case with imaginary stalkers
would think, isn't it?

Wacky 1980s romantic yuppie comedy *When Harry Met
Sally* addressed the question of whether men and women can
ever be friends without having sex. My experiences with
Poopy Partridge have made me wonder whether fans and
their idols can ever truly be friends without the fans getting
weird.

15

The Child-Fucking Class Warrior

According to the UN Convention on the Rights of the Child's definition of what exactly constitutes a child—"every human being below the age of 18 years"—writer **Mark Ames** is by his own admission a child-fucker.

But hold tight—I'll get back to that in a minute.

The evidence suggests I was a huge inspiration on Mark as a writer. Other writers have suggested that he lifted his confrontational style from me. He also stole *ANSWER Me!*'s "Your Mother is a Whore" graphic and used it on the cover of his Russian newspaper the *eXile* (edgy capital "X" there). He blatantly plagiarized my graphic "legend" guide to serial killers from *ANSWER Me!* and reproduced it as "Death Porn Legend" in the same paper. He was so entranced with me, he even put my face on the cover!

What's clear is that he knew about me long before I became aware of him, which only happened when he started running his neck about me.

In his writing, he casts himself as a bold and brave proletarian warrior. He claims to have lived in "poverty" yet somehow was miraculously able to blithely globetrot as a sex tourist without any discernible source of income. He slams people with "rich family connections," denies he was "born into a rich family," and once criticized someone for behaving "like some thrill-seeking rich kid committed to little more than his own whim." In print and on TV, he has habitually bloviated on behalf of "the people" and "the poor" against "the rich," "the wealthy," and especially "the oligarchs."

Yet he was born and raised in the absurdly wealthy California coastal town of Saratoga—pretty much Ground Zero for the mega-villainous "1%" against which ersatz class warriors are always fulminating. He attended private school and is allegedly the son of a millionaire San Francisco lawyer. His elocution is that of a rampagingly effeminate sheltered rich kid, which wouldn't be a sticking point if he wasn't constantly trying to convince the world that he's a "real man" who's waging class warfare against "the rich." Despite his champagne-socialist posturing, he wouldn't have a clue what it's like to be working-class even if the ghost of Emma Goldman walked up and took a shit on his head.

His entire existence is a trust-fund Disneyland of projection. His every word and self-consciously "gonzo" action suggests he's riddled with wealth guilt and trauma envy.

Naturally, he has repeatedly accused *me* of trying to hide my "upper-class" upbringing. When challenged to defend that allegation face-to-face, the lawyer's son from a posh Cali coastal town has hidden from the plumber's son who grew up in a brick row home outside Philly every time.

Through self-admitted rampant amphetamine use leading to endless stretches where he'd smell conspiracies in his nostril hairs, Mark seems to have consumed enough speed to power a paper airplane to Pluto and back. He appears to be stuck in some form of late-stage amphetamine psychosis that has induced delusions leading him to pin the slightest wisp of deviation from progressive political orthodoxy on the evil handiwork of the billionaire Koch brothers, who funnel money at right-wing and libertarian causes.

In February 2011 I wrote an article about Wisconsin teachers who'd crammed their cheese-laden, sweatpants-swaddled bodies into the State Capitol Building as they chanted and wailed over minimal budget cuts. "Jim Goad sucks Koch," Ames Tweeted, alleging that I'd either sold out to or fallen under the sinister ideological spell of the Kochs' propaganda machine. He also rc-Tweeted someone else's comment urging that I should be sent back to prison:

> **ameslevinelist**
> *Jim Goad sucks Koch: From "Redneck Manifesto"*
> *to anti-union waterboy, you've come a long way,*
> *baby!*
>
> **svirgula RT by ameslevinelist**
> *@ameslevinelist Jim Goad is a libertarian swine.*
> *Should be sent back to prison. Thanks for this.*
> *21 Feb*

Back to prison, eh? OK, "real man," look me in the eyes and try saying that.

I left a comment on his site challenging him to back up his words. Rather than publishing my comment, he completely rewrote it but left it in my name, so it reads as if I'm confessing to "selling out" for a blogging gig as well as "getting old" and "beating up chicks" and having lost relevance since the 1990s. He also published my phone number, which led to a couple harassing calls from his handful of readers.

I was not working for any Koch-funded outlet, nor endorsing Republicans, nor trying to get a gig on Fox News as he accused me. Yet he was appearing on MSBNC shilling for Democrats and writing for a magazine that received funding from billionaire leftist puppeteer George Soros. While working for a giant multinational corporation, he accused me of selling out to corporate interests.

Over the next few years, he would repeatedly bring up my age, although Mark is a mere four years younger than I am. If you take decades of amphetamine use into account, his innards are likely centuries older than mine.

Though he also repeatedly called me "obscure" and "unknown" and "irrelevant," by most reliable measures of fame I am more famous than he is. A failed screenwriter, he kept accusing me of being a failed actor. Fame has never been a concern of mine, but apparently it is crucial to him. Yet he loses to me even in the swimsuit competition.

Again—and let's say it together this time—"projection."

He also repeatedly accused me of hating Jews and being a "white power" advocate, but he never proved bold enough to try and defend his words. Over the years Ames would claim that he was a "real man" who was "fighting power" while depicting my friends and I as empty poseurs. Still, he could never somehow bring himself to call me a coward to my face, no matter how many times I offered him the opportunity. An ex-coworker of his pegged him as a quintessential keyboard warrior:

Brave behind the computer screen, he's actually shy in person, with an inferiority complex towards extroverted partyers.

Writing in *The Moscow Times,* another ex-associate bemoaned Ames's "lack of balls" for being afraid to admit that he cowered behind a pseudonym when writing about his real-life rape of a girl he'd left "bleeding and crying." He also portrayed Ames's "brave journalist" routine as empty posturing:

In any case, [Ames's] self-righteous, Serpico-style whistle-blower, fearless-investigative-reporting shtick is just a pose. For one, they're just inaccurate—a grave mistake when you're setting yourself up as the arbiter of journalistic ethics.

More on the rape thing in a minute, along with further elaboration about the child-fucking. Be patient. I'll get to those, I swear. But yes, Mark Ames *is* an accused rapist *and* a self-admitted child-fucker. And if you were to Google-bomb the world with this information from now unto perpetuity, you would be telling the complete truth and thus staying snugly within the bounds of ethical journalism. But I want to make it clear that I'm not suggesting you do that, OK?

Several other writers—including Glenn Greenwald, who is currently perhaps the world's most respected journalist—have called out Ames for paranoid false inferences and propping his arguments up on logical fallacies as if they were crutches. Greenwald referred to one of his articles as a "shoddy, fact-free, and reckless hit piece." Even *Nation* editor Katrina vanden Heuvel, who as a sheltered limousine liberal should feel a natural blood kinship with Ames, felt obliged to apologize for his sloppiness. Breitbart.com did a long article unspooling a toilet-paper-roll-length list of Ames's journalistic fuckups. But rather than respond directly to any of this fact-niggling like a true journalist would, Ames's default reaction was always to mock his antagonists personally. It was as if he was incapable of responding in any other way.

For years, he wrote comments and posted them in my name on his website, though I hadn't tried commenting there since he rewrote my first comment.

If he had shown the rudimentary honor to try to defend his initial accusation like journalists are supposed to, I would have whipped him like Kunta Kinte in a debate and that would have been the end of it.

Instead, he kept harping on the crime that landed me in prison, just as so many keyboard antagonists had done for thirteen years and counting at that point. He eventually added the lurid flourish that I had crushed Anne Lyin's eye socket. Later he upped the ante and accused me of breaking her skull. The official hospital report says nothing of the kind—in fact, it says "No internal trauma identified"—but don't expect a bold and righteous "journalist" such as Ames to ever retract such a clearly libelous statement. The truth is that he's a blind ideologue rather than a journalist but is far too stupid to know the difference.

Since he insisted on taking the low road, I returned the courtesy.

In the anthology to the *eXile*, Ames declared the book to

be "a work of nonfiction" and that "all of the characters and events depicted in the book are real." Writing under his own name rather than a pseudonym, Ames described an event that occurred in his early 30s when he became extra-aroused to learn that a "homely" peasant girl that he would ply with alcohol before fucking and discarding was 15 rather than 16:

> "Dude do you realize...do you know how old that Natasha is?" he said.
>
> "Sixteen?"
>
> "No! No, she's fif-teen. Fif-teen." Right then my pervometer needle hit the red. I had to have her, even if she was homely. I sat down next to her on the couch and fed her another double martini with pineapple juice, and asked her to take off her clothes now...."

He also wrote that "Her cunt was as tight as a cat's ass." In 2000, the *Chicago Reader* cited that passage with some measure of alarm, yet Ames did not object nor try to claim it was written as satire or under a *nom de plume*.

Also in 2000—which can safely be described as the peak of Ames's skimpy notoriety before he began his long, yawning decline—his ex-associate Owen Matthews accused him of being a rapist in a *Moscow Times* article:

> It's that lack of balls that is most disappointing. Why, for instance, keep up the fiction that "Johnny

Chen," the eXile's controversial pseudonymous club reviewer, actually exists? "Johnny Chen" is—surprise, surprise—Mark Ames. I know because I was present during many of Chen-Ames' sordid adventures, which were subsequently written up to the horror of the eXile's more straight-laced readers. I can only assume that Ames—wacky, speed-guzzling, on-the-edge Ames—couldn't face owning up to an infamous (and hilarious) piece describing how he rapes a devushka he drags out of a club and into his apartment.

And here's Ames's pseudonymous account of that "hilarious" rape:

…hurried her down to a taxi, ran her home, up my stairs, and into my apartment. The whole time she was begging me to take her back, to be careful, she was drunk, bla-bla-blah … After we were through, I had no idea what to do with her. She was bleeding and crying. As for me, I was depressed. I'd just shot a load large enough to repopulate North Korea. So I walked her over to my balcony, and held her in my arm, leaning her over the ledge.

"Throw her over," Johnny Jr. advised me.

"What?"

"You know you want to," he said. "Just pick her up and throw her over. You'll feel better, I promise."

Suddenly, after a dozen years, that, too, became "satire." See, in *The Moscow Times*, when his *ex-friend* wrote that Ames didn't have the balls to own up to being a rapist, even *that* was all, well, *satire*, OK? I mean, how many times does that have to be explained?!

I found it all so wondrously gonzo, I let his employers know about the child-fucking and the rape accusation. I Twitter-blasted the fuck out of these facts for a few weeks running. After thirteen years of having people throw my crime in my face to try to silence all other discussion, I could finally throw a fastball made of shit right back at one of them.

At first, Ames acted like it was not a big deal, that he had already written about it in a book and that his employers knew all about it. Then, according to a third party, he tried explaining he'd been partially passed-out while fucking the fifteen-year-old, which makes one wonder how he was able to gauge her vaginal torsion. Then he claimed it was all satire—that he was only playing a part, even though he wrote about it in his own name in a book that claimed to be a work of nonfiction.

So either he lied in the book or he lied about it subsequently. Either way, goodbye journalistic credibility forever! TRUTH TO POWER!

Around this time I started getting harassed on my Facebook group by someone who called himself "Cedrick Delaney."

Problem was, I did not witness any of the harassment, since

"Cedrick" had blocked me. He had railed at me for a solid week before another group member asked me what Cedrick's deal was. I had no answer, because I hadn't seen any of the posts. Cedrick was too cowardly to let me see the posts where he was calling me a coward. Cedrick, who had posted several videos by Pet Shop Boys on my group wall, sent my Norwegian friend Lasse Holmberg Josephsen an avatar where Mark Ames's face was Photoshopped onto the head of Pet Shop Boys' singer.

I had another admin ban Cedrick from the group, whereupon commenced what at the time of this writing has been nearly three years of email and Facebook harassment by a trio of imaginary personages whose behavior, writing style, and repeated focus on certain subjects (Fox News, Gavin McInnes, Joel B. Pollak, me being a washed-up emblem of the 1990s who now works for peanuts) and key phrases ("like father, like son," "real men like me who fight power," "teeny tiny turkey twats") strongly suggest that they are all shell accounts Mark Ames is using to harass me.

> *Date: Sunday, September 11, 2011 11:08:38 PM*
> *Subject: dance puppets dance*
> *"Chen was the perfect representation of the West's rapacious mission in Russia…"*
>
> *Betcha didn't see that coming eh? I suppose it never occurred to any of your IQs that the 15-not-16 year old tale was…allegory? I got you good Goad. And there's nothing you can do about it sucker.*

Obviously someone was sweating liquid methamphetamine about the child-fucking thing. The problem is that his child-fucking passage was written under *Ames's own byline*, not the Johnny Chen pseudonym. "Chen" was the one who wrote about raping a girl and leaving her bleeding and crying. Mark Ames may have pioneered a new literary genre, that of "non-fictional allegory."

For nearly two years, "Cedrick" sent me countless emails calling me a stupid, retarded, dumb, irrelevant, old idiot who was stuck in the 1990s—apparently because I didn't gullibly swallow Karl Marx's scribblings from the 1840s. I did not respond to any of them and eventually shunted them off to a "stalkers" folder in my email program so I didn't have to look at them.

Another fake profile on Facebook that went under the name "Richard Currly" stalked me to accuse me, as luck would have it, of stalking Ames:

> ### Richard Currly:
> *Jim Goad is stalking you like a fangirl Ames, he still can't get over having his sorry ass handed to him—so he's gonna get his big rich Koch brother to come and beat you up Ames, so you better watch out cuz it's coming soon! On a really big website. Cuz you know, having bad things written about what a pig you are Ames—that's like going to destroy your career! Yeah it's true—especially if all these bad bad things are on a BIG website and it makes Ames even more famous, then yeah, that's going to totally hurt Ames' media career.*

Cuz you know how this stuff works! Just wait till this BIG website publishes all the bad stuff Ames has done—Ames's career is totally over, man! Bad publicity is career death in our business. everyone knows that!

Try make a big deal of things if you want, Jimmy, but Once your Koch-suckers read a few of the deviant lines that you've published, you'll go back to being the same old pathetic 90s nobody. Good night Jimmy.

Then, when I gently insinuated that it was obvious "Richard Currly" was Mark Ames, he suddenly lost his bravado, offered up his pink belly, claimed to have cancer, and quoted Longfellow:

Jim Goad: *Adderall apparently makes people refer to themselves in the third person.*

Richard Currly: *I was diagnosed with bowel cancer on Monday.*

There are things of which I may not speak;
There are dreams that cannot die;
There are thoughts that make the strong heart weak,
And bring a pallor into the cheek,
And a mist before the eye.
And the words of that fatal song

Come over me like a chill:
"A boy's will is the wind's will,
And the thoughts of youth are long, long thoughts."

That was the last I heard from "Richard Currly," but "Cedrick Delaney" continued harassing me. One day on my Facebook group, someone asked whether Ames was still bothering me. I wrote that he was needling me under a pseudonym and added a shout-out to him because I knew he was probably lurking—"Hi, CD!"

Within moments, "Cedrick Delaney" sent me a conciliatory email wherein he also insinuated he would die soon, just as "Richard Currly" had done upon being identified:

> **From:** *Cedrick Delaney*
> **Date:** *Saturday, September 1, 2012 8:44:46 PM*
> *Subject: Gone on long enough…*
> *Come on now, Jimmy…*
>
> *Although a lion in the face of danger, you're a self-proclaimed skittish little boy who does most of – no wait – all of his talking from behind a keyboard.*
>
> *I won't be around a couple years from now; you'll be gone shortly after. The world will remember neither of us – although you never made it to Vanity Fair, Jimmy!*
>
> *But seriously, just mortal thoughts these days: it*

was all juvenile nonsense. I bare [sic] you no ill will, and I never really did. In life, it was a luxury to be your "enemy." I've always respected you as a man, and admired you as a writer.

Cherish your time.
CD

As craven as that was to proffer a desiccated fig leaf while hiding behind a pseudonym, at least I figured it was the end of the harassment and that the mentally diseased speed freak would go lie under a eucalyptus tree and quietly die.

Less than two months later, "Cedrick" started tossing poison email darts at me again. So I decided that every time he pestered me with another email, I would post something online about him being a child-fucker and accused rapist—and I'd use the pseudonyms "Cedrick Delaney" and "Richard Currly" to do it.

Otherwise, I didn't make another peep about Ames until March of 2013, when his fey poofter of a new publisher offered a golden setup line about "date rapists" on Twitter. I alerted the publisher that he may very well have a date rapist on his staff. Again, Ames tried to fob it all off as "satire" while accusing me of breaking a woman's skull for threatening to "out" me as a homosexual rich kid.

Methinks the lisping countess doth protest WAY too much.

In August of 2013, while Ames's new website venture was failing and his publisher was openly panhandling for new investors, I received an email from a "Nathan Pearson" quibbling over a passage in an online news feature that I edit.

At first I figured it was really someone named "Nathan Pearson" contacting me with a genuine factual concern. After hearing his case—basically, he was drawing a false inference but didn't realize it—I told him that I quoted a government document accurately but if he thought I hadn't, he was free to leave a comment calling me out for what he thought was a mistake.

"Nathan" refused, instead calling me a "coward," a "retard," and "stupid, stupid, stupid." He also launched in again with the "real men" and "teeny tiny turkey twat" patter and how I'm supposedly still bitter that I never went to acting school, all of which made me strongly suspect it was the lonely failed screenwriter Mark Ames reaching out into the darkness yet again to digi-touch me.

I addressed him as "Mark" and told him he could have avoided wearing the "child fucker" and "rapist" jackets for life if he'd merely had the decency to debate me about Wisconsin's teachers in the first place.

He wrote:

> *Why would i debate a I guy who smears teachers*
> *for chump change?*

And I replied:

> *The more salient question is, why would you con-*
> *tinue harassing that same guy nearly three years*
> *after the fact? Obviously I got way under your*
> *skin. Since you dodged the issue at hand and*
> *focused on the bitch-beating—like, um, a real*

journalist does, right?—I made sure you'd wear
the rapo jacket for the rest of your life—using your
own words against you. And it worked!

Yes indeedy-do, it did. The meme has sprouted wings and taken on a life of its own. From time to time I'll run across people online who are sinking their teeth into Ames's hairy ankles and won't let go of the "rapist" and "child-fucker" themes. But now when he tries to play it off as satire or the false accusations of a woman-beating anti-Semite, they point out that he wrote about it himself in a work of nonfiction.

On Twitter, an ex-paramour of his recently insinuated he'd been abusive toward numerous ex-girlfriends:

> **moe tkacik @moetkacik 10 Jan**
> *when will someone get the balls to ask Mark Ames*
> *why none of his abused girlfriends has gone postal*
> *on him yet*

Hilarious! But *satirical*—in an entirely nonfictional sort of way!

16

The World's Most Inept Blackmailer

Experience has taught me that when someone calls you the genius of your generation, you should immediately cut off all contact with them and move to another continent.

I generally have a very high regard for Asian intelligence and Asian culture. Sadly, what appears to be the dumbest Asian on Earth became one of my most devoted fans and committed stalkers.

Fail Dim is a Korean American who served time in the Iraq War and may have had his brains irrevocably scrambled as a result. Either that, or his eggshell had already been cracked long before then.

Among his cornucopia of problems is a face that must be regarded as an unfortunate anomaly of nature. It is a disagreeable face. An unpleasant face. A face that scares dogs and small children. It looks like a moray eel sucking a pickle. Life cannot be easy for anyone with a face such as that. As far as I know, his face was not disfigured in war. It appears he was born with that face. It is faces such as his that lead skeptics to question God's existence. No loving God would give a person that face.

Yet his personality is even more grotesque than his face.

Perhaps his face is so shockingly uncomely to prepare you for the burbling cauldron of roach feces that is his personality.

To avert most of his problems, he would need an entirely new face and a completely new personality. And that's just for *starters*.

Instead, it appears he has spent most of his waking hours for the last two-and-a-half years having a pathetic and delusional one-way "feud" with me. I imagine I also occupy much of his dreamtime.

He had emailed me back in 2009 calling me the genius of the current generation. I thanked him for the compliment but was wary, seeing how those who are most effusive in their praise usually become the most hysterical in their condemnation once you gently ask them to maintain their distance.

He became a member of my Facebook group and almost immediately began sucking up a disproportionate amount of air there. This is the problem with public forums, just as with public saloons—there's always one loudmouthed nitwit who ruins everyone's fun.

He wasted no time in defaming the Muslims he'd been sent over to murder in the Middle East, referring to "ragheads" and "that shit stain known as the Muslim world." He also made several comments claiming that white people are stupid pussies.

That wouldn't be relevant except for the fact that his astronomically inept Internet vendetta against me is based on the concept that I am a racist—an anti-Semite in particular. Not only that, his Machiavelli-with-Down-Syndrome extortion scheme was based on the assumption that I tremble in fear that the world might one day become aware of the evil that lurketh within my Jew-hating heart.

Fail is an obsessive philo-Semite who smells Nazis in the very *kimchi* that he nibbles. He also has such flesh-crawling fondness for Jewish girls, I'd suggest that the State of Israel take out a class-action restraining order against him on behalf of all daughters of Judah.

I've wondered why this tragically homely and magnificently unlikable Asian male held such loudly articulated hatred for "white nationalists" or "white supremacists" or "Nazis" or any of the groups to whom he tried to shackle me in dimwitted acts of guilt by association. Although he claimed he was "damn proud" of being Korean, he refused to tolerate the idea that any white person could dare to so much as claim they're not ashamed of being white. I suspect he may have been mocked or rejected by a white person—most likely a girl—and decided to blame all whites rather than, again, his repellently unsalvageable personality.

Like Rupert Pupkin in *The King of Comedy*, he appeared to feel that since he "knew" me through my writing, he was entitled to a lifelong friendship with me as an equal—he would later claim that we had been "friends" and "buddies," although I never considered him one. He even wrote that we had been "fans" of one another. Like prior serial harassers such as Anus Large and Anti-Semitic Steve, he would often wrap his compliments in insults and misguided career advice cloaked as "concern" for my well-being. On the Facebook group, he was always trying to catch me in a mistake and always failing. That gets tiresome after the hundredth try and hundredth failure.

But he was not Rupert Pupkin. He was, and remains,

Rupert Pup Dim. And with the war-vet angle, there's an element of Travis Bickle from *Taxi Driver*. He is therefore also Travis Pickled Radish.

One day on my Facebook group someone posted a news story exemplifying the crazed censorious humorless Orwellian crowdsourced lynch mob into which latter-day political correctness has metastasized, a culture of public shaming and snitching and hysterical mob-mentality moral panicking far worse and totalitarian than the Red Scare I had witnessed as a child. A commenter asked me how I thought PC had gotten so entrenched.

I recommended a book called *The Culture of Critique* by Dr. Kevin MacDonald. You can read the book and think whatever you'd like to think about it—I don't have any emotional investment in your opinions and thus won't stalk you for years if you disagree.

The Culture of Critique is an exhaustively documented tome that examines the notion of "anti-Semitism" through a prism of evolutionary group psychology. MacDonald argues that open immigration, multiculturalism, and political correctness were primarily Jewish group survival strategies against monolithically white cultures. He does not for a moment delve into the sort of bug-eyed, foam-flecked, hate-drooling obsessiveness stereotypically associated with "anti-Semitism."

I calmly tried explaining all this to Fail, but he would always respond with dumb, flailing incomprehension over dozens of increasingly tedious emails. He started patronizingly suggesting that evil Jew-hating Nazis had hypnotized me while in prison. He acted as if he was only trying to help me break out of my Hitlerian fog before it was too late and I became forever in thrall to the Dark Side. This mentally ill insect actually felt qualified to lecture me.

Anyone who has the most rudimentary understanding of me knows I'm antisocial and I don't join group movements. The last group I joined was the Boy Scouts. That's why I don't identify as "liberal" or "conservative" or "white pride" or anything else. For fuck's sake, I never even seek to *hang out* with people. At base I'm a skeptic and I think modern race hysteria fits all the qualifications of a classic moral panic, so I fixate on that. I guess it's my psychological damage for being raised Catholic. My brain naturally latches onto taboos.

But he was completely missing the point every time. I said if he wasn't going to read the book, then he should shut his twisted face and not bother me about it.

He persisted in bothering me about it anyway, and he also grew increasingly belligerent toward other commenters on my Facebook group and on Taki's Mag, a site for which I write and edit. I warned him on the Taki comments that if he kept harassing people, I was going to ban him.

He pecked out some angry comment to me. I banned him just as I'd promised.

He would proceed to deal with this rejection far worse than any woman I've ever dumped. And he immediately saw fit to bring up my exes and my prison stint, as if they were the matter at hand rather than his personality.

Date: *Wednesday, May 11, 2011 at 9:35:05 AM*
Subject: *2.5 years in prison, huh?*
It certainly got to you.

I sighed and wrote him a farewell letter. It would be nearly a year before I would respond to him again:

> *From: Jim Goad*
> *Subject: re: 2.5 years in prison, huh?*
> **> It certainly got to you.**
>
> *Yeah, brain surgery, too.*
>
> *And the specter of dying at any moment from brain- or heart-related problems while I have a two-year-old who I love like crazy and depends on me to raise and protect him.*
>
> *You know how all this got to me? It made me realize that my time may be limited, therefore I've become absolutely intolerant of wasting time with anyone who annoys me. It may not matter to you, but as far as these things go, I've been unusually tolerant of you.*
>
> *The reason I brought up my wife is because she hardly ever looks at the Facebook group but had skimmed it over the past couple days and asked me, "Who the fuck is this guy? He's annoying as shit!" A lot of other friends whose opinions I value had expressed the same sentiment very recently.*
>
> *Feel free to speculate why you've annoyed me or anyone else if it helps you save face or feel you've achieved some sort of victory.*

The only thing you could do to make me feel that I was wrong for cutting you loose is to quit with the juvenile taunts about prison and suchlike. Otherwise, you're only confirming my gut instincts.

I won't reply to any further emails. I've been through this routine more times than I care to remember, and I've never regretted cutting the cord on someone.

Have a nice life. I'm done.

Note the reason I gave for blocking him—because he's intensely annoying. He would then go on a sustained and insane rampage to prove me absolutely correct.

Subject: *Re: 2.5 years in prison, huh?*
Date: *5/11/11 1:27 PM*
To: *Jim Goad*
Well. I'm fine with you moving on with your life. I must move on with mine.

It kinda bums me out that this is it....I think you've become a bitter old man you never thought you would become when you were younger.

And the fact you just blocked me out goes to show you have some serious vendetta problems.

Subject: *When you bullshit. You don't get sympathy from me.*

Date: 5/11/11 10:00 PM
From how I look at it, maybe Debbie and Anne
were saying a lot more truthful things about you
than how you play it off as. Right on dude. You
really are a coward.

Three days later, when I still hadn't responded, he sent a detailed apology and blamed his medication regimen—rather than any willful, self-directed actions—for his behavior:

Subject: I am crazy AND stupid. And I should
apologize and thank you.
Date: 5/14/11 11:57 PM
I think preventing me from typing any more com-
ments from Taki Mag and the Jim Goad group
page is probably the best thing you've done for me.
I have not taken experimental medication I have
been prescribed lately and right now it is experi-
mental. I believe I have gone thru some manic
episodes for a couple of months now and the best
thing for me to do is stay away from the internet
so I won't type things out which I may later forget.

Hopefully I will not bother you any further but I
hope you do read this email and don't think I'm a
complete asshole. I don't think I'm at the best
mental and emotional state to start reading about
politics and such at my life. I hope the best of luck
for you and your family and I don't want any
more stress upon your life. I also hope to find the

*help I need so I won't go around getting in fights
with people constantly.*

*I realized I had a problem when I yelled at some-
one for walking her poodle because pedigree dogs
promotes inbreeding. For whatever reason my
emotions took over even though I should keep my
mouth shut.*

*Again, I hope you read this. And please watch out
for people spying on your group page on Facebook.
Me and you both are delusional but there are crazier people out there trying to undermine you for
whatever reason. And to be honest I've come to
realize Kevin B. MacDonald makes a couple of a
good points. But again, all this government control
talk is REALLY unhealthy for me.*

*Best of luck and keep on writing. You always be
funny, sharp, and honest. Peace out.*

He later told someone else that one of the "crazier people out
there trying to undermine" me was "Cedrick Delaney," the
man I'm 99% sure is 1%er Mark Ames. Cedrick had contacted
him and encouraged him to keep antagonizing me.

I imagine Fail bit his lip and sat on his hands for another
four days until, like Anne Lyin', he just couldn't keep himself
away from me anymore:

Subject: *One last flaw to point out. I can't help*

notice you like to defend the Confederacy....
Date: *5/18/11 4:53 AM*
*Weren't they pro-slavery? Which means they are
pro-multi racial society? I find a flaw in that logic
when you think you're so brave in railing against
multiculturalism. Especially when you're preach-
ing to the choir.*

Such is the curse of being a writer. You have to deal with
brain-damaged scrotal lice making false assumptions and
then leaping to false conclusions that should break their legs
for jumping so foolishly. I never wrote a word "defending" the
Confederacy, and only a cretinous heartbroken serial harasser
could claim the Confederacy was a "multicultural" society. Yet
there he was, proud little yellow rooster, puffing his chest and
acting as if he'd FINALLY caught me in a mistake.

I had already endured MONTHS of these imbecilic
"GOTCHA!" moments from him, and he persisted in shooting himself in his cherry-sized nuts over and over and over
again. He failed to realize he had no point to make and was, in
essence, only lashing out emotionally like a teenage girl.

There are some people you can't argue with because they're
too stupid to realize they can't argue.

But he would persist in having a one-way argument, yelling
into the abyss and labeling it a "feud."

And just like the slimiest of stalkers, he would attempt to
drag everyone in my periphery into his psychotic maelstrom.

He began co-stalking author Gavin McInnes, a founder of
VICE magazine who writes for two of the websites I edit. Most

of Fail's harassment of Gavin involved phone calls and text messages:

May 14, 2011 6:26 PM
I am a very sick man. And I don't have a lot of friends.

Sep 3, 2011 7:46 PM
My mom told me my dad was drunk when I was conceived and that's probably the reason why I'm so weird. Not joking.

When Gavin began distancing himself, Fail started spreading a rumor that years ago, Gavin had fallen asleep drunk at a party and someone took a Polaroid where a black guy placed his dick in Gavin's unconscious mouth. I suspect that because Fail thought we were all Nazis, we would get our American Nazi Party membership cards revoked and lose all street cred with our white-nationalist fanbase if this information were revealed. Nobody likes a Nazi with a black dick in his mouth, especially his fellow Nazis.

Gavin says he thinks Fail may have misrepresented a story about a published photo where a *VICE* photographer is snorting a line of coke off a black guy's dick. Either way, it's dumb to blame someone who passes out drunk for anything beyond passing out drunk. Gavin says that since his own wife is a fag hag, if she heard that there's a picture of him with a black dick in his mouth he would probably get laid more often.

None of this mattered to Fail. Far beneath the squirming mealworms that were eating his brain, he decided he had sufficient material to blackmail both me and Gavin. He was going to "out" me as an anti-Semite and Gavin as a guy who passes out drunk and then goes ahead and unconsciously permits a black guy to put his dick in his mouth. He seemed to delude himself that this was why we didn't like him—because he had blackmail material on us—rather than what Occam's Razor would dictate, which is that he was unlikable.

Fail started sending out repeated mass emails to what seemed like everyone ever associated with the Street Carnage website, trying to explain his "side" of the imaginary "beef" between him, me, and Gavin.

He also started harassing Lasse Holmberg Josephsen, a funny and eminently likable member of my Facebook group. These messages from Fail are from from a private Facebook discussion between Fail and Lasse:

> *Hey you wanna see a picture of Gavin McInnes with a black cock in his mouth?*
>
> *I have it. Just wanted to throw that out there. You lost an ally.*

Note that he says he has the photo in his possession. This is important.

Fail continues talking about black cock:

> *I know how to play some games, ready? I wait until Gavin's kids turn 18 then send them a picture of their father with a big black cock in his mouth. Don't fuck with the master of fuck fuck*

games... Don't know if you knew Gavin's "friend" Dash Snow. But he got this guy [to put] his cock in Gavin's mouth while he was passed out. I've got time on my side....If you saw your dad with a big black cock in his mouth. How would you feel?...I got dirt on those two like you don't even know. You don't even know me....When Gavin passed out during a night of drinking Earsnot put his dick in his mouth and Dash Snow took pictures....He's a black guy. He's got a big dick....I just wanted you to know that about Gavin and if he ever pissed you off you can hold that against him....Pretty sure he doesn't like the fact he had a big, black dick in his mouth....Actually I want A LOT of people to know that. Especially his friends....You need to give people a chance and a fair hearing. You need to look at both sides of the story.

For months, Gavin and I ignored the mass emails.

After five months of my silence, Fail set the bar even lower:

> **Subject:** *Since I can't leave comments on Taki anymore I just wanted to tell you this.*
> **Date:** *10/21/11 4:33 PM*
> *How about you go to Paris and get murdered.*
> *Fuck you.*

He was referring to the murder of my deaf brother Bucky, who was stabbed and strangled to death in Paris in 1969.

But Fail didn't mind dragging Gavin's kids and my murdered brother into his incomprehensibly stupid revenge
scheme.

After five *more* months of uninterrupted emails, he decided
to start posting on the Taki site using different screen names
that mocked my brother's death. He and his ground-up corpse
of a brain warned me of this nefarious plan via email:

> **Subject:** *By the way...*
> **Date**: *Tue, 6 Mar 2012 11:43:39 -0800*
> *When you get more accounts blocked on Taki*
> *thinking they might be me, the usernames might*
> *get more exciting. Just letting you know.*
>
> **Date:** *Wed, 7 Mar 2012 12:19:51 -0800*
> **Subject:** *possible usernames for people*
> *HaHaBuckyDied BuckyInFrance BuckyDeaf-*
> *BlindDumb PoorOldBucky BuckyGiveYouGood-*
> *Time 5DollarBucky RapingBucky*
> *List goes on and on.*
>
> **Date:** *Wednesday, March 7, 2012 3:15:29 PM*
> **Subject:** *Blocking users for their names and suspi-*
> *cions they are a certain someone*
> *It only gets worse from here from thinking up*
> *usernames. Ya know, that right?*
>
> **Date:** *Wednesday, March 7, 2012 3:27:43 PM*
> **Subject:** *All KINDS of NEW USERNAMES!*
> *GhostRapingBucky BuckyLikesRape Bucky-*
> *SucksSatanDick DickSuckingBucky Shanked-*

Bucky
commenting without approval!

Date: Wednesday, March 7, 2012 3:36:54 PM
Subject: More usernames
BuckyGangRape BuckyGoadStabathon Bucky-
GoadGoesT oFrance BuckyLearnsSomeFrench It
goes on and on.

He had also started contacting Taki's daughter Mandolyna, my boss at takimag.com. He insulted her father and brother. And he made sure she knew that I'm a wife-beating anti-Semite and that Gavin fell asleep drunk once, whereupon a black guy stuck his cock in his mouth.

Then, nearly a full year after I'd bid him goodbye and he'd continued his nonstop harassment of everyone tangentially related to me or Gavin, he sent Gavin what most legal jurisdictions would probably deem a blackmail threat:

Date: April 28, 2012 9:59:19 AM EDT
Subject: I'm willing to negotiate.
I can go far with a lot of things I know about you
and I what I can prove but we can come to terms
where we can mutually benefit. You interested?
Because you can continuously give me the cold
shoulder until I do things that will force you to
respond. So what will it be? Hell. I can save Jim
Goad's reputation while I'm at it. I know he has
some emails from you that you can't play away as

a prank so I KNOW you have to be in good terms with him.

So what can we do to come to a compromise?

Ahh, the "cold shoulder." Isn't that what it's really all about?

He repeatedly alleged that the only reason Gavin and I are friends is because I possess blackmail material against Gavin. It appears that Fail can't conceive why anyone would be someone else's friend without some sort of ransom or blackmail scheme being involved.

Gavin and I decided that rather than go to the police, the best course would simply be to publicly document Fail's year-long jag of uninterrupted and unprovoked harassment. He had even posted our phone numbers on his Twitter account and phoned both of us repeatedly. We documented it all on Gavin's website, Street Carnage.

Someone in Street Carnage's comments ragged on us for preying upon a "mentally ill" person. I shed no tears. Whatever he winds up doing is entirely his fault. I don't buy the "mentally ill" alibi for a second. He'd chosen to press SEND for a solid year, then copped out and blamed it on his "meds." All we'd done for a year straight was ignore him. But he wouldn't go away. As another friend of mine that he also harassed would tell him, there's a difference between being mentally ill and being an asshole, and he was both.

Fail, who apparently checks that site every five minutes, immediately emailed me. I sent him back what was to be my last contact ever with him:

Date: *Tuesday, May 1, 2012 6:40:44 PM*
Subject: *Re: Jim I still have the same twitter account...*
Here's the official record of me telling you to never contact me again.

Thus began Phase 2 of his Dumbo Jihad: A relentless fusillade of emails and phone calls begging for us to remove what we'd posted about him. The batty ex-soldier even waved a little white flag—yet in the clumsy and self-defeating style of so many of these imbeciles, he managed to toss in a violent threat while asking for a favor:

> **Subject:** *You got your revenge Jim, do you feel better now?*
> **Date:** *Tue, 22 May 2012 00:03:00 -0700*
> *You and Gavin got me back. You three actually (including Lasse) got me back real good. Just take my contact address off in the emails from the website.*
>
> *By the way, if I ever end up in Norway, I'm gonna find Lasse. I will find him and whoop his ass....*

We continued posting documentation of his harassment, noting the irony that someone who had tried so hard to "expose" us had scurried like a frantic *cucaracha* from a bare lightbulb the minute we merely reprinted his own words. He got it stuck in his cracked mind that we would freak out and try to suppress information about us that was either untrue, didn't bother us, or that we'd POSTED PUBLICLY already…yet here he was, sweating spicy red drops of *kimchi* juice that we'd given him a dose of his own medicine.

Date: *Saturday, July 14, 2012 3:13:56 AM*
Subject: *Please remove my contact information off your site.*

I would remove everything I posted about you guys on my site and will cease future posts if you remove all your defaming posts about me and especially my contact information. I will never contact you guys again. I would go so far as avoiding typing your names ever again. You will never receive an email or a call from me. You won't see any edits on your Wikipedia pages by me. I won't email any of your colleagues or your friends ever again. I will shoot them an email if they want to cease all contact with me they just give me the heads up. Pretty sure everyone I still correspond with at this point haven't told me to fuck off.…

> *Anyway, I will wipe myself away from your radars under a simple condition. This I will all do if you remove my likeness off the web page known as Street Carnage. I will be a ghost and will wipe myself away from your universe as long you get rid of my likeness off your website. You have my word.…Otherwise I will persistently pester you two to remove my likeness from your website.*

Date: *Wednesday, July 25, 2012 8:45:55 PM*
Subject: *We disappear from each other's lives. How about this?*

I will never mention you guys ever again. I want everything off Street Canage of my likeness. My picture. My name. No one will think I have ever dealt with your website nor that you have ever dealt with me.

I will never edit or touch everything or anything with you guys. I just want everything off the Street Carnage site of my likeness. My name. Everything.

Anyway, I'm planning to email your brother and your wife to apologize telling them I'm sorry about telling other people that TRUE story about you having Earsnot put his dick in your mouth while you were passed out and that other time Nicky Katt told me you woke up with a condom up your ass. I will explain to them in vivid detail and it's I am very sincere in my apology.

I hope we all get out of each other's lives and move on. Jim is an old man with serious health problems so he will eventually croak... Please remove my contact information and my likeness OFF your website. And I will stop bothering you. I'll be a ghost and disappear. And we all want that, don't we?

Awww, da poor widdle ghost was feelin' trapped! We were not going to bend to the demands of some psychotic jerkoff who'd spent a solid uninterrupted year trying to fuck with us. Unlike his repeated harassment via personal contact, what we were doing was also entirely legal…and, I may add, quite fun.

We documented his harassment in an additional three posts on Street Carnage. Until now, those four posts would constitute the entirety of our "feuding" with him—merely documenting what he'd done for a solid year.

He *continued* harassing us, now flipping the script and claiming that *he* was the victim of stalking and harassment. Technically—you know, in the *real* world—we were making no personal contact with him while he continued emailing and phoning us.

He'd also obsessively read my Facebook group and the minute I banned someone, he'd contact them and try to persuade them to join him in his sacred and all-consuming cyber-blitzkrieg.

Waltzing delusionally through a hall of mirrors, he went so far as to accuse us of trying to befriend him on Facebook, prank-calling him, and posting his whereabouts:

> **Date:** *Friday, September 7, 2012 8:30:42 AM*
> **Subject:** *Enough with the fucking prank calls*
> *I don't know who you guys got to call me at shitty hours of the night with blocked numbers but I'm gonna change phone numbers now because of you guys.*
>
> *I was hoping I wouldn't have to deal with you guys anymore but for whatever reason you guys won't let up…Stop fucking making fake profiles on facebook to "add me as a friend" or "subscribe" to*

*my feeds on facebook to fucking stalk me you shit
tard. Just fuck off otherwise with the prank calls
and posting my whereabouts on the internet.*

Then, on Christmas—more than 19 months after he strapped
on his rubber-duckie sandals and began his lonely scorched-
Earth one-man march to the sea—he warned of an even more
diabolical attack to come unless we removed the posts from
Street Carnage. He generously gave me two days to comply
with his demands:

> **Date:** *Tuesday, December 25, 2012 7:52:07 PM*
> **Subject:** *Merry Christmas.*
> *Listen, I know I've given you some pestering
> emails but the only reason why I bother is because
> you know why. I still get prank calls from people
> so I'm just gonna press on until you remove the
> defaming and libelous material from Street Car-
> nage. By the way, I also figured out some things
> about your wife. So I'm gonna go ahead and start
> with phase 2 with my little internet fight between
> me, you, and Gavin. You have about two days.*
>
> *Hopefully by then you will remove everything of
> my likeness off Street Carnage and we will cease to
> interact.*

Silly, silly me—I was unaware there was any "interacting" at
all. I hadn't realized I was the one whose behavior was main-

taining this relationship that he desperately sought to escape. How did I fail to discern that I was the one standing in the way of this breakup? It soon became obvious that I couldn't get over him and was stubbornly maintaining contact with him by not contacting him. Why couldn't I stop ignoring him and just leave him alone? Why didn't I understand? Why didn't I obey?

He made it clear that *he's* the one who's burning bridges, NOT the 500-odd people who rejected him and that he subsequently harassed.

He waited three days for me to accept his gracious offer, and when I didn't respond, he came out yet again, his three-inch guns a-blazin'. He initially directed his bold and frightening debate challenge to me, then rewrote it a couple times and included Gavin. He claimed that he'd been "reluctant" to do this, but that our constant imaginary harassment left him no other choice.

The gist of his debate proposal:

> *Let me start off this debate with a simple question for you Mr. James Thaddeus Goad: Have you ever hit the mother of your child in anger?*
>
> *I know you were a wife-beater. I'm just curious if you still are currently beating your wife, Shannon. I know you gave Debbie Goad two black eyes….How will you explain to your son how much of a good father you are when you're the type of guy who likes to smack the old lady around?*

So have you Jim? ANSWER ME! Have you ever hit your current wife??

So let's go at it peckerwood. What are you afraid of? What's the worst that can happen debating me on the internet? You think I'm just gonna travel through Ethernet cables across the country and punch you? I'm typing this from LA homeboy. You're reading this in Georgia.

Still, after all these years, this is all that any of my castaways had in their arsenals to throw at me—the "wife-beating Nazi" thing which, to my surprise and eventual delight, had led to more action with chicks than I'd ever imagined possible. There was even a buxotic black stripper in Portland who sought me out and had sex with me just because someone told her I'm a Nazi. And for that night alone, I wasn't going to tell her I wasn't.

Mind you, you have to have women *around* you in order to beat them—at the very least, they need to be within arm's reach. I suspect that very few women have ever so much as willingly been in the same *room* with Fail. I think he may still be a virgin.

A long time ago he had sent me a jealous email asking about why I got so much pussy after getting out of prison.

Well, to begin with, it's because my face and personality are far better than his. And I'm known for far more than stalking people who block me.

I ignored his challenge to have a "debate" based on loaded questions, whereupon he began harassing dozens of members of my Facebook group one by one, begging them to post the challenge on his behalf. If they did not comply, he would accuse them of being a "spy" for me and Gavin.

One by one, he also Tweeted at my Twitter followers to read his exciting and truth-digging challenge.

Highlights of those Tweets:

1 MORE THING: I agree with 98.99% of Jim Goad's worldview politically & socially. It's not about politics. It's more personal.

[The debate] can go anywhere. From his ties to white power groups and the fact he still gets involved with domestic violence.

Getting to know someone you admired is a mixed blessing. Sooner or later you will become familiar with his or her faults.

A man I once admired never said he was a saint but it was irritating to see him surround himself with people that did.

I also happen to know Goad has direct ties with white power groups who think Jews rule the world.

But I would be more impressed if Jim Goad owned up to the fact his wife's white power. And his weirder thoughts on Jews…

You think he worked out all his violent anger issues?

You know his wife's a Nazi, right?

The "his wife's a Nazi" thing came from her Facebook URL. It includes the number "88," which in neo-Nazi circles is shorthand for "HH," AKA "Heil Hitler." It had actually been her roller derby number instead, but I wasn't about to break my silence and tell him he was barking at the wrong poodle owner again. And even though he bumblingly and inaccurately tried accusing me of libel, the mere passage "the fact he still gets involved with domestic violence" is 100% slam-dunk legally libelous.

Everything he does is stupid and wrong and stinks of sour, scaly, peeling feet. What's worse, he will be stuck with himself for the rest of his life. He will never be able to crawl out of his own awful skin.

I think it was Socrates who said if you can't win a one-way argument, just pretend that you can read your opponent's mind. He continued accusing me of being afraid to air my True Jew Views but that he, in his noble quest as the Yellow Knight of Israel, would ensure "the truth will prevail about Jim Goad and his real thoughts about the matter." This, despite the retardedly simple idea that if I were afraid of making these heinous ideas known, I wouldn't have *posted them on Facebook for all the world to see* like I did, which is what caused him to have a scrotal aneurysm in the first place.

But with stalkers, things don't *have* to make sense. What drives them is not logic, but their girlishly emotional urge to destroy a hero that hurt them, however passively.

Here was his most telling Tweet of them all:

Sometimes I like to think I bruised someone's ego so much "unfollowing" him on twitter that he went ahead and killed himself.

My God, my God—ye who sitteth comfortably nestled in the heavens above wearing a Snuggie and sipping a mug of hot cocoa with those little marshmallows floating atop it—one could poke an eye out on all that projection.

He started spelling his first name differently in what I assumed was a desperate attempt to avoid the fact that our articles about him are among the first results when you search his real name online.

In March of 2013, after another round of accusing me of being a "libelous charlatan" who hated Jews and still beat my wife despite the fact that she's apparently a Nazi, too, he sent me a lighthearted email about small Asian penises as if we were old chums and everything else was water under the bridge.

During yet another mass-mailing that was mostly CC'd to people who had no involvement and no apparent interest in his one-way "feud," he wrote this about me:

He may or may not have joined a white prison gang during his time in jail.

At some unspecified point between ages 7 and 9, I may or may not have also been a unicorn. And throughout his adult life, Fail may or may not have been a member of NAMBLA. He may or may not constantly suck black cocks, too. But he appears to have black cock on the mind. It's amazing that his brain doesn't implode from all the giant black cocks resting on it.

He never could talk enough about penises, whether it was tiny Asian ones, black ones in Gavin's mouth, or his allegation that I have white nationalist fanboys standing in line to suck my cock. Cock was a constant theme with him. Cock, cock, cock. Cock around the clock. Numerous women have suggested he's absolutely gay for me and would come running back wagging his tail...sorry, his *Fail*...if I merely snapped my fingers. Come to think of it, he did once email me to say a picture of me wielding an axe was "sexy." And he also confessed to keeping a fake Facebook profile as "a gay dude."

After the small-Asian-penis email, I didn't hear directly from him for another seven months—during which he tried befriending anyone who said anything negative about me. He even contacted my wife to try and convince her I was fucking other women. It probably tortured him to think that a woman-beater could snag all that tail while he sat alone, stroking his paltry member. Then he emailed me to rehash the Gavin-had-a-black-cock-in-his-mouth story again. He's still sticking by it.

Sad—so very, very sad is he. It turns out that despite his claims that he possessed the picture in question—the smoking gun of his entire blackmail scheme, or rather *blackcockmail* scheme, against Gavin—he was lying. He never had it and never even saw it. Desperation drove him to begin begging on his blog that if anyone had the photo, they should send it to him:

But seriously though, I know a number of his friends who told me Dash Snow took pictures of Gavin passed out while this really scary big black guy named Earsnot put his dick in Gavin's mouth....

By the way, if anyone out there has those pictures by Dash Snow please feel free to contact me ASAP and just post that shit on the internet for everyone to enjoy.

I just want to say all these allegations are 100% true. I'm pretty sure just because I can name the names of people in his circle who told me about the Dash Snow incident.

"[T]hese allegations are **100% true**. I'm **pretty sure...**" In other words, "I'm *pretty* sure they're 100% true, but not, like *100%* sure or anything." This, after claiming he had the smoking gun in his possession.

Lying liar who tells lies and libels while he's lying about other people being libelous liars!

He has two Twitter feeds where he re-Tweets his own Tweets hour after hour and day after day and month after month. I don't think I've ever seen loneliness quite this deep, yet I've never seen it so entirely earned, either. His loneliness is the result of pure hard work and merit.

He recently contacted Lasse out of the blue to accuse him of being my spy. He threatened to beat Lasse up should he ever visit Norway. He claimed that worse was in store for

Gavin, because, well, even though nobody asked him, Fail hates Gavin even more than he hates the woman who molested Fail as a child.

If it's true that a woman molested him, well, at least *one* woman in his life has touched him.

Thirty months of effort—and counting—merely to provide me with all this free comedy material. Peel away the Jews and the Nazis and the black cocks and the wife-beating and the endless hours spent harassing the heroes that snubbed you, and all that's left is a fundamentally atrocious personality.

When life hands you a lemon, make lemonade. When it hands you a cockroach, shine a light on it.

17

The Folly of Revenge

And so it continues, this odd religious ritual where I turn away would-be acolytes and they cry sour grapes forever.

There was the triple-chinned alcoholic housewife who offered me money and free trips and free advice until I gently told her no thanks, whereupon she privately needled me and publicly harassed every girl in my periphery for months. I think she may have sobered up and quieted down once she realized I have tons of documentation where she complains about the time her husband beat the shit out of her in a cab…how he hasn't gone down on her in ten years and didn't even fuck her on her wedding night…how she and I are like Tracy and Hepburn…how she wants to marry me…and how she continued pathetically chasing me after I told her we had no future.

There was the talentless "transgressive" cartoonist who humbly approached me claiming he was my fan but then launched several DDoS attacks on my website once I blocked him. And after the dust cleared and my site went back up—*voilà!*—he *still* had no talent.

There's the obsessive commenter who claimed my writing saved his life. He left an estimated 3,000 comments in one month on Taki's Mag and was banned as a result. I wasn't even the one who banned him. He then left a psychotic screed aimed at me on his own website:

> *You won the battle, Goad, but you're going to lose the war.*
>
> *In my opinion Karma has a way of sticking it to ex-cons, especially ex-cons with anger manage-ment problems. In my opinion someday somebody is going to say something to you that you'll misin-terpret, you'll grab the handiest deadly weapon—glass ashtray, gun, baseball bat, knife—and then you'll kill the mofu in a frenzy of chemically untreated bipolar rage … after which you'll resume your career of doing life in prison on the installment plan.*

Take a deep breath and listen closely.

If haven't flown into a rage after these endless needlers who've been poking at me over the past fifteen years, I obvi-ously have greater composure than any of these jilted abor-tions. My kung fu is far stronger than all those little grasshop-pers combined. I've endured trials by fire that none of them could ever handle—especially if they freak out to this degree over simply being blocked online.

As you read this, someone somewhere in the continental USA may be donning diapers, grabbing an assault rifle, and driving toward me.

That's not how you get revenge.

Here's a little story about revenge.

My first marriage ended due to infidelity. The lowest thing I'd ever done in my life—far worse than ever hitting anyone—was to cheat on a cancer patient that I loved. The cheating had started before she came down with cancer, but it continued after her diagnosis.

After we got divorced and she was still bald from chemotherapy, I'd visit her every week to deliver money and free weed. During one visit as I sat on the floor of her house and she sat perched on the couch, she looked down on me and in her caustic Brooklyn accent meekly said:

"Jimmy, rather than ever even *thinking* about ever cheating on you, I would rather have had an axe down come down from the sky and cut me in two."

She expressed her pain so nakedly, I wanted to die from remorse. I wanted the floor to open up and swallow me. I felt horrible about myself. She had gotten her revenge.

But about a year later, drawn into a sick media circus surrounding the arrest that landed me in prison, she started piling on. She went on a dedicated campaign to "expose" me, yabbering online and contacting everyone remotely associated with me to not only talk about all the bad things I'd done, but to severely exaggerate them. For instance, I must have blacked out the time I threw a refrigerator on her. She also called my case manager in prison and told him that I'm a murderer who will certainly try to kill her upon my release.

Suddenly, I had no remorse toward her. Here she was, consciously seeking to harm me. So the score was settled. We were even. I no longer felt bad about anything I'd done toward her.

That's the problem with revenge. It backfires. And it drags you down to the level of your target—even lower, because they rejected you first, and you'll never even get back to Square One no matter how hard you try.

I'll never understand why some people deal with rejection by going on campaigns to prove themselves 100% worthy of being rejected. None of these elaborately retarded vendettas made me regret cutting the cord on any of these losers. In fact, it merely justified my suspicions that they didn't deserve my friendship or trust. Their behavior ensures that I don't regret rejecting them—only ever being polite to them in the first place.

Through it all, they remain who they are. Nothing will change that. And throughout their variegated revenge schemes, they never magically acquire talent or charm.

Water seeks its own level. Theirs just happens to be that of a toilet.

The happy ending to this story is that it gives me great cheer to realize there are people in the world far more miserable than I am. For all they tried to make me suffer, their suffering is a type that I will thankfully never know. In their quest to make my life a living hell, they only reveal they are screaming for a sip of water amid flames and pitchforks. Their worm dieth not, and the fire is not quenched.

Sure, most of these psychos may have been drawn to whatever they perceived, accurately or otherwise, to be psychotic about me. But my main mistake here was stooping low enough to even permit them access to me. My sin here is not malice but naïvete. I've finally learned the perils of casting pearls before fans. If that makes me a dick, well, suck it.

Social media is the wrong place for the antisocial. The brain-sucking deer ticks who antagonize me are idiots, but I was an idiot for interacting with them in the first place. I've always been smart; the problem is that I've never been too wise. I've realized it's masochistic to spend so much time arguing with people I hate, people who'll never understand me no matter how slowly I type. As a friend recently told me, I worry about the wrong people, the ones I don't even respect. It's true that I never cared whether these fans-turned-stalkers *liked* me, but I worried far too much about whether they *understood* me. It took over a half-century of being alive to realize I can't make dumb people smart and I'll never be able to make annoying people likable. When I'm on my deathbed, I doubt I'll fret that I didn't spend enough time engaged in flame wars.

I've adopted a Zen approach to it all. If someone insults you online and you don't read it, are you truly insulted?

So if I didn't accept your friend request, now you know why. I've shut down my Facebook group and although I'm staying on Twitter, I've vowed never to check who's taunting me. I will no longer allow myself to be sucked into this sick black electro-vortex. I'll let my writing speak for itself, and if people don't understand it, that's no longer my problem. I've wasted enough of my life stubbing my toes while trudging through fields of morons. I'm punching out my time card in the headache factory and walking out into the sunshine.

Thought Catalog, it's a website.

www.thoughtcatalog.com

Social

facebook.com/thoughtcatalog

twitter.com/thoughtcatalog

tumblr.com/thoughtcatalog

instagram.com/thoughtcatalog

Corporate

www.thought.is

Made in the USA
Columbia, SC
18 May 2023